"Watch out, there's a contagio~~n~~ has certainly tasted the presenc~~e~~ Reading *Worship 365* will crea~~te~~ experience God's presence and grow in your life of worship. David's insights and exhortations will move you, not just to the next step, but on a journey of next steps."
— Gerrit Gustafson, worship teacher (worshipschools.com) and writer (*The Adventure of Worship*)

"As a young worship leader myself, I really appreciate Edwards's maturity and leadership. His godly example of a true worshiper's heart comes through in his writing. My first read had me underlining and highlighting like a madman. This is a fantastic teaching tool!"
— Matt Brouwer, singer/songwriter, www.mattbro.com

"David Edwards is simply passionate about perpetually pursuing the heart of God. His insight about worship shifts paradigms for worship leaders and worshipers alike. If you want to go to a deeper place in relationship with and worship of Almighty God, this book will get you well on your way!"
— Craig Adams, worship pastor and music producer

"My friend Dave Edwards, driven by a passion for His presence, combined with diligent study of the Word, has written a great book on worship. There are many books that focus on technique, trends, and cultural relevancy, but precious few that take us into 'the secret place under the shadow of the Almighty.' This book speaks well of the transformational aspect of worship, inspiring the believer to go into that place of His presence."
— Caleb Quaye, New World Music Ministries, CA

"When we first met David M. Edwards, we knew he was called of God in music. He was different, open to what God wanted him to do. One day we escorted him to a church service where he was to minister—just a normal church. The service was according to the program until Reverend Edwards came to the piano. In a matter of minutes, we actually saw and felt the

presence of the Lord come, and people literally fell on their knees, including us. God has used this man to change the environment of the ordinary to real worship. As you read *Worship 365: The Power of a Worshiping Life,* you, too, will desire to be in His presence every day of your life."
> — Tim and Betty Cornett, evangelists/missionaries
> to Bulgaria www.cornettministries.com

"David Edwards drives straight into the core questions many of us have been asking about worship for years, albeit privately and a bit furtively. *Worship 365* is a tender guidebook, leading us right into the nucleus of worship itself—an extravagant, no-holds-barred love relationship with the living God."
> — Sally Morgenthaler, founder, Sacramentis.com;
> president, Digital Glass Productions

"No matter where you stand today, David Edwards will equip you for the journey to a deeper place in your worship through *Worship 365.* The power of a worshiping life is truly revealed in the pages of this book!"
> — Jessica Wolstenholm, senior director of marketing,
> Myrrh Records

"My friend David Edwards writes *Worship 365* as a shepherd, teacher, minister, worshiper, edifier, encourager, writer, psalmist, and prayer warrior who is truly 'called' of God. This book will give you an insatiable appetite for worship and impassion your soul to communicate the gospel."
> — Alan Shacklock, producer

"In an age where worship has become something mysterious and complicated, it is refreshing to find a book that brings worship back down (to earth). In *Worship 365* you are sure to find wisdom for walking in a practical, yet intimate lifestyle of worship."
> — Michael Farren, worship leader and lead singer
> of Pocket Full of Rocks

"My friend David has managed to grapple with the truths of worship in a way that welcomes everyone to enjoy the fullness of the Christian life! This is a book for those of us who want to live for Jesus, a practical step into learning and living out our passion to follow Him. Whenever I'm with David, I'm always struck by the love he has for Jesus and for others around him. In this book the very same fragrances permeate throughout these pages! There's no room for halfhearted worship, God wants every bit of us!"

— John Hartley, worship songwriter/producer

"In *Worship 365: The Power of a Worshiping Life*, David M. Edwards helps us move our focus upward and into God's holy presence. A powerful and inspiring book that challenges us to have a deeper personal relationship with God."

— Regi Stone, worship leader,
www.experienceworship.com

"Why did people sit on the edge of their seats when Jesus talked about heaven? Because that's where He came from! When I think of my friend David M. Edwards and *Worship 365*, I'm encouraged that edge-of-the-seat books are still being written. Thank you, David, for taking us to where you have been."

— Gregg Johnson, speaker/author
and founder of J12 Ministries, www.j12.com

"It is undoubtedly a formidable task for anyone to write an informed book on worship. Even more daunting, when we understand that the spiritual power in the book's textual fiber is only realized through the consistency and quality of the author's own personal worship and living. As it relates to both matters, here is my report: the cornerstone of what David M. Edwards writes and lives is authentic love for Jesus, passion, and excellence."

— Greg Nelson, songwriter/producer

"David Edwards takes a complex and seemingly overwhelming subject matter, that of worship, and breaks it down for the worshiper. Written in his informal and natural storytelling style, Edwards helps unpack the mystery of worship, taking apart misconceptions that limit our understanding of the power of praise. Then he helps the reader to grab hold of the promises that God has for His people through the process of becoming a worshiper yielded to His presence. With *Worship 365*, David Edwards has done what very few writers have been able to do,

write a substantive book about worship that is both enjoyable and informative!"
— Julie Reid, executive editor,
Worship Leader magazine

"In the pages of *Worship 365*, David M. Edwards outlines the various aspects of worship and the ways to experience the power in a worshiping life. With practical insight and moving inspiration, David writes in a clear, understandable manner that encourages Christians to passionately delve into the concept of worship—a subject that indeed touches the very heart of God."
— Tim Marshall, senior vice president of artist relations,
World Label Group (Word Records,
Fervent Records & Myrrh Records)

"David M. Edwards's book, *Worship 365*, serves as a timely reminder that praise and worship is so much more than an event or style of music. Our highest calling of ministry is the worship of our creator, and the means whereby we accomplish this are virtually limitless!"
— Dallas Holm, songwriter,
Praise Ministries, www.dallasholm.org

"What a wonderfully biblical perspective on worship. My spirit bears witness with what David M. Edwards shares here. It is truly refreshing indeed. I found that I was very aware of the presence of the Lord even as I was reading!"
— Mike Weaver of Big Daddy Weave,
Fervent Recording Artists:
www.bigdaddyweave.com

"I commend to you [David Edwards], his ministry, and his writing, for it is only out of the abundance of the heart that a man speaks. David is a man with an abundance of worship for the Most High in his heart. It is not the man who defines the substance and quality of his worship; it is the substance and quality of his worship that defines the man. I hear in the pages of this book the heart of a man of God."
— Anthony Chapman, senior pastor
The Rock Church, York, England
www.rockchurch.org.uk

365^W

worshipthreesixtyfive

David M. Edwards

365W

worshipthreesixtyfive

the power of a worshiping life

B&H
PUBLISHING GROUP
nashville, tennessee

ISBN: 978-0-8054-4367-7

Published by B&H Publishing Group,
Nashville, Tennessee

Dewey Decimal Classification: 248.3
Subject Heading: WORSHIP \ CHRISTIAN LIFE

Unless noted otherwise, scriptural passages are from the Holman Christian
Standard Bible, © 1999, 2000, 2002, 2003 by Holman Bible Publishers,
Nashville Tennessee; all rights reserved. Passages marked NIV are from the
New International Version, copyright © 1973, 1978, 1984 by International
Bible Society; NKJV are from the New King James Version, copyright ©
1982 by Thomas Nelson, Inc.; and AMP passages are from the Amplified
Bible, copyright © 1954, 1958, 1962, 1964, 1965, 1987 by the Lockman
Foundation.

This book is dedicated to my parents,

LOUIS AND WANDA EDWARDS,

for teaching me how to be a worshiper.

Duo Seraphim

Duo Seraphim clamabant alter ad alterum:
Sanctus, Sanctus, Sanctus Dominus Deus Sabaoth:
Plena est omnis terra gloria eius.
Tres sunt qui testimonium dant in caelo:
Pater, Verbum, et Spiritus Sanctus et hi tres unum sunt.

Sanctus, Sanctus, Sanctus Dominus Deus Sabaoth:
Plena est omnis terra gloria eius.
Gloria Patri, et Filio, et Spiritui Sancto:
Plena est omnis terra gloria eius.
Amen.

RESPOND, 3RD NOCTURN AT MATINS
ON TRINITY SUNDAY; FROM ISA. 6:3

Two seraphim cried one to the other:
Holy, Holy, Holy, Lord God of Sabaoth:
The whole earth is filled with His glory.
There are three who give this testimony in heaven:
The Father, the Word, and the Holy Spirit,
and these three are one.

Holy, Holy, Holy, Lord God of Sabaoth:
The whole earth is filled with His glory.
Glory be to the Father, the Son, and the Holy Spirit:
The whole earth is filled with His glory.
Amen.

Contents

Foreword: xv
Acknowledgments: xix

Introduction: 1

Part 1 / 5
Chapter 1: What Is Worship?   7
Chapter 2: Worship: A Two-Way Street   21
Chapter 3: Worship: Hungering for God's Presence   31

Part 2 / 51
Chapter 4: Putting On Praise   53
Chapter 5: The Power of Praise   65
Chapter 6: The Sacrifice of Praise   80

Part 3 / 93
Chapter 7: The Way In   95
Chapter 8: The Presence and the Presents   109
Chapter 9: The Promise of His Presence   123

Part 4 / 135
Chapter 10: Throne Room Encounters   137
Chapter 11: The Fruit of Our Own
                    Throne Room Encounters   146
Chapter 12: Power to Worship   161

Final Thoughts: 175

About the Author: 181
Notes 183

Foreword

§ § §

What does it take to become a true worshiper, to experience a relationship with God that transcends anything one has ever known? Who do you need to be, and what do you need to do? Is there one program, formula, or "package" God prefers? In your heart of hearts, you wonder if you are capable of getting close to God. You read the Psalms, and you long for the kind of intimate bond David enjoys with the Lord, one that he expresses so vitally—even viscerally. Perhaps David had a gene you lack. Perhaps there are people in your life who seem to have it. Like David, they can't get enough of God's presence. They seem to have a knack for putting their wants and needs aside. Their natural tendency is to focus on God's work in the world, and God's desires, not their own. Does one have to be born with this gene, or can a worship "default" be developed?

You muse about this. One of the problems is that there is so much "noise" about worship these days. Yet, it is just that. Noise. A cacophony of hype where worship's essential "melody"—God's surpassing glory and worth—is easily obscured. So much of what passes for worship may actually be self-worship. You think of the last dozen praise choruses you've sung, and, with notable exceptions, most seem to fit into the category of all-about-me ballads sung in two keys: nice and pretty.

As one who wants to go deeper in your life of adoration, that kind of worship doesn't help. You may not know much, but you have figured out that you're not interested in worship that's about you. You've been around enough blocks to know that if God's not bigger than you you're in deep trouble. Neither are you interested in nice and pretty. That combo doesn't resemble your life at all, which is more mess than masterpiece most days. And so you want to cut through the nice, the pretty, and the self-focused to arrive at an experience described in Isaiah 6. Like Isaiah, you want to bare your soul and be transformed. But worship as it has become in new-millennium America feels more like bearing one's own image than baring one's soul, and its goal seems more about staying the same versus being transformed.

What is real, unabashed worship? You're aching to know. So you wait to find out more. One of these Sundays, it's all going to come together. The worship leader at your church is saying all the right words in between the songs. Surely he knows. And here's where you bump into yet another reality: many worship leaders don't have a clue what real worship is. Even more alarming: it may not matter that they don't have a clue. In more settings than most of us realize, all a savvy job candidate needs to snag a worship leader position is a set of pretty good guitar skills, a "golden-boy" look, and a couple dozen jargon-saturated worship monologues.

Lately you've begun to wonder about the emphasis placed on the cosmetic of your church's worship services. That activity alone takes up over half your church's budget. You ask, "Does worship only happen if you have U2-talent status? How far does the cool factor really take people into God's presence?" The other thing you're wondering is, "Does worship only happen inside four walls at a specific time and place?" You love your church's worship services. You love new forms of worship—video, bands, contemporary music—but you wonder if there is more to glorifying God than what goes on between 10:00 and 11:15 a.m., one day a week. You wonder about what it means to adore God by yourself, at the office, in your family, with your friends, taking care of strangers, spending time with the needy. You're sure Jesus' worship looked more like that—an outside-the-building thing—but you've never read anything on the subject.

And here is where David M. Edwards's book is at its best. Instead of rehashing the cosmetics of a worship service, Edwards drives straight into the core questions many of us have been asking about worship for years, albeit privately and a bit furtively. Instead of an academic treatise or a pragmatic how-to-wow-your-church-visitors tome, Edwards offers a tender guidebook, taking us straight into the nucleus of worship itself—an extravagant, no-holds-barred love relationship with the living God.

Anyone can spout worship platitudes. Only a true worshiper—a frequent traveler—can actually picture transcendent reality, meticulously painting the landscape of intimacy with God. And that is what separates this book from the hundreds of worship volumes on the shelf. From the first page, it is obvious that Edwards's worship shoes are journey-worn, that his paths to God are the well-beaten roads of the hungry seeker. Yet, there is not a hint of self-congratulation in these pages. There is only the persistent, shepherdlike invitation into a journey that has become to him a familiar, exquisite wilderness: the lifelong glorification of the only One worthy to be glorified.

> — Sally Morgenthaler
> Founder, Sacramentis.com
> President, Digital Glass Productions

Acknowledgments

§ § §

I wish to express my sincere appreciation to my publisher, David Shepherd, for being open to the things of God and open to me. To Ken Stephens, Gary Terashita, John Thompson, Jean Eckenrode, Lisa Parnell, and the entire B&H family my sincere thanks for all you've done for me.

To my literary agent, David Sanford, and the entire staff at Sanford Communications, Inc., thank you so much for your guidance and perseverance. I would in particular like to thank my editor, Elizabeth Jones, for a phenomenal job and for working so quickly.

To my manager, Glenda J. McNalley, I wish to express my deep appreciation for her tireless efforts on my behalf and for her unwavering friendship.

To my beautiful wife, Susan, thank you for your love and for standing by my side; I love you. To our wonderful blessings, Tara, Elyse, and Evan, Daddy loves you so much.

As I look back over the years, there are so many people to thank who believed in me and encouraged me when no one knew my name. They saw something in me worth sowing into and told me to follow my dreams. My life is a collective response of all of those who took the time to invest in me, believe in me, and be God's wisdom to me. I would especially like to thank the following, for I am a better man because you have touched my life:

Mom and Dad, Dan and Michelle Edwards, Margaret Elizabeth Becker, Louis and Stella Edwards, Dolores Smith, Margaret Becker, Greg Nelson, Craig Adams, Sally Morgenthaler, Chris Hauser, Melissa Riddle, Danielle Kimes, Janine Van Beek, Dr. Richard Dresselhaus, Dr. Herbert Prince, Dr. Jack Hayford, Dr. and Mrs. Tim and Betty Cornett, Harlan Rogers, Danniebelle Hall, Beverly Brafford, Roy Hicks Jr., David and Carolita Fraley, and Rev. Anthony Chapman.

Introduction

§ § §

*I*had my first experience with the presence of God when I was five years old. Arriving home from my half-day kindergarten, I usually ate lunch with my mom and baby brother, then hurried off to play Batman—or better yet, Indian chief. Then, on the days my short attention span quickly ran out, I would resort to spying on Mom.

This was one of those days. I knelt quietly on the wooden floor outside my parents' bedroom. Pressing my ear against the door, I heard a familiar sound—the voice of my mother, talking to God in prayer.

Suddenly I felt as if "something" reached underneath that door and wrapped itself around me while she prayed. As I felt the hair on my arms stand up and my spine begin to tingle, I had an acute spiritual awareness that something altogether good was happening all around me as my mother worshiped God with tender words of love and adoration.

What was it that I felt? What was this wonderful thing that showed up every time my mother had her prayer time? What could it have been that left such an indelible touch upon my heart at an early age? Something was going on in that room that was not of this world. Something impossible to put into words. A connection between this world and the next, between heaven and earth, was being made.

My mother had set aside time to spend with God, to tell Him how much she loved Him, how much He meant to our family, and how much we trusted His Word in our lives. I couldn't hear God talking audibly to my mother—the only voice I heard was hers—but He was speaking to her and I knew it. The words of praise that filled the air told me that my mother was communing with the living God.

As I grew older, I had no trouble associating that "presence" with the Lord Jesus Christ, for it seemed to show up quite regularly when we prayed and worshiped Him at church. I even remember sensing this "presence" when the pastor gave an invitation for people to meet Jesus Christ as their personal Lord and Savior. I saw amazing things happen when Jesus was welcomed and cherished, both in my personal life and corporately. It seemed that everywhere I turned there it was again—that "presence." It was and is this same presence that arrested my attention as a small boy, crouched outside my parents' bedroom door.

As a teenager, I began to put it all together when I read, "But You are holy, enthroned on the praises of Israel" (Ps. 22:3). I began to understand that God's presence is all around us all the time, but it is when someone intentionally taps into that presence that it takes on a whole new dimension from our perspective. In other words, when God is enthroned in our worship, His manifest presence appears.

If God's presence appeared under the Old Covenant in very real ways, how much more should it appear under the New Covenant of grace, as the priesthood of believers offers the sacrifice of praise and thanksgiving to Him? Jesus spoke of this dynamic in Matthew 18:20: "For where two or three are gathered together in My name, I am there among them." No matter what the meeting, no matter what the gathering, as long as the agenda is "in My name" He has promised to show up!

During my college years, I was fortunate enough to attend a university in the city where my grandmother lived. I spent many weekends at her house, willingly partaking of her southern home cooking over the cafeteria food on the other side of town.

On one such weekend I lay awake in her guestroom, unable to fall asleep. I could hear a faint voice, mixed with the sound of crying, echoing down the hallway from her bedroom. As I got up to make sure she was OK, I could see down the hallway into her bedroom. She was kneeling beside her bed, Bible open in front of her, hands open toward heaven, worshiping the Lord.

I quietly slipped back into my room, not wanting to disturb this holy sight. I lay in my bed and stared up at the ceiling, remembering myself as the five-year-old boy, listening to my mother's time with the Lord. God's presence seemed so near, almost tangible. I felt so blessed and thankful for my spiritual heritage, as well as the privilege of observing my parents and grandparents worship the Almighty (cf. 2 Timothy 1:5–7).

Perhaps these glimpses of my past give you an idea of where I am coming from. Our different experiences growing up have shaped who we have become, and I believe these times were instrumental in forming who I am today and how I have come to understand this multifaceted thing we call "worship."

God's holy presence, that glory that shows up wherever He is honored, worshiped, loved, and welcomed, is needed today more than ever. Thus, the purpose of this book is to look into this holy subject, worship, within the contemporary church of the Lord Jesus Christ. When we use the word *worship*, what do we mean? Is worship just an activity that we involve ourselves in a couple of times a week, or is it also a biblical principle for everyday life? Why would the Holy

Spirit want to empower believers to worship? Is worship a time and space event or not? With these thoughts in mind, God's Word as our foundation, and His Holy Spirit as our guide to all "truth and righteousness," let us look into a subject that touches the very heart of God.

Part 1

It Is You

Words & Music: David M. Edwards*

Verse 1:
You, who move the mountains
You, who calm the seas
You, who made the heavens
You, who first loved me

Chorus:
It is you, you, Lord Jesus
It is you
It is you, you, Lord Jesus
It is you

Verse 2:
You, who bled and suffered
You, who paid sin's price
You, who died to save me
You, who gave me life

Chorus:
It is you, you, Lord Jesus
It is you
It is you, you, Lord Jesus
It is you

Verse 3:
You, who sit in glory
You, who'll never die
You, who'll come back for me
You, who'll split the sky

Chorus:
It is you, you, Lord Jesus
It is you
It is you, you, Lord Jesus
It is you

*2001 New Spring Publishing (ASCAP) / Nail Prince Music (ASCAP) Admin. by Brentwood-Benson Music Publishing, Incorporated / Van Ness Press, Inc. (ASCAP)

Chapter 1

What Is Worship?

§ § §

*"The chief end of man is to praise God
and glorify Him forever."*
—WESTMINSTER CATECHISM OF FAITH

*T*he Bible contains no less than six hundred references to worship—and uses at least eighty-seven different Hebrew and Greek words to describe praise and worship. Worship is an activity that takes place throughout the pages of God's Word. It existed before the earth was made and will be a part of the new heaven and earth that is yet to come.

Worship is the most important ministry of the church of the Lord Jesus Christ. Her worship *to* Him must come before her ministry *for* Him. Worship helps us individually and corporately to keep God first in our priorities. It helps us focus on Him and remember that it's all about Him—not about us. Worship helps us to stay centered in a world that is constantly out of focus with what is important.

When you mention the word *worship,* it can conjure up all sorts of images in people's minds. Understandably, people are generally afraid of what they don't know—what is outside their realm of experience. For instance, if someone is in a worship service where the worship leader or pastor is encouraging those present to raise their hands, they may feel a bit self-conscious about it if they have never done it before. Just because they have never done it before does not make it unscriptural—it's in the Bible—but they were never taught that it's OK to raise their hands. People perish for lack of knowledge, and people's worship experiences can be dull and dry for the same lack of knowledge. Don't let your potential to have a powerful worship encounter with the living God be hindered because of a lack of knowledge! I challenge you to join me in the adventure of finding out what God's Word says about worship.

The purpose of everything in this book is not meant to be exhaustive (there's no such thing), nor do I care to sit and parse Greek and Hebrew words and overwhelm you with intellectual arguments. There may be those who consider themselves an expert on worship or have differing opinions, and that's fine with me. I am just a man who knows something about the presence of God—only because I, like billions of others, have experienced it and I hunger for more and more.

Growing Up in Worship

The other day I thought to myself, *I want to grow up before I grow old!* I want to grow up and grow out in my understanding and receptivity of God's Word in me and to me. I don't want to remain where I'm at—I want to move ahead with Him.

The children of Israel walked in circles for forty years! God still loved them and provided for them, but they never got anywhere. God has loved me, too, while I've walked in spiritual circles: circles of doubt, circles of unbelief, circles of my own will. How I thank Him that His love for me never changes and that He has consistently loved me through those times.

But I hunger to discover what God has for me. I refuse to walk in circles, seeing the same scenery, hearing the same old lines, getting nowhere fast, while the God of all creation stands ready to do something fresh in me. I must fight the temptation to walk in my little spiritual circle instead of following Him into the unknown, into the new, into the heights that I've never climbed. What am I afraid of? He holds my hand.

> We worship a God who is not only received by faith but can be experienced in a very intimate way.

Another very important point as we study worship is the subject of *truth*. Biblical truth sets us free to understand about the pure worship of the Holy. Jesus said that God is looking for those who will worship Him *"in spirit and truth"* (John 4:24). In order for truth to set us free, we need to know it.

"If you continue in My word, you really are My disciples. You will know the truth, and the truth will set you free" (John 8:31–32). It's the truth you know that sets you free. Knowing the Scripture is knowing truth, but knowing Jesus is also knowing truth, for He alone is truth personified. Therefore, we should continually hunger for God's Word because our understanding of it, led by the Holy Spirit, will set us free to be who He has called and created us to be. Jesus loves us where we are, but He wants us to move on—He's calling you to the mountain! Don't fear, just take off your shoes and go!

Our hunger for more of Jesus in our lives will also lead us into a deeper walk with Him, which in turn will begin to set us free through every dimension of our being. We worship a God who is not only received by faith but can be experienced in a very intimate way. The God of Israel still speaks, still heals, still sets free, still abides, still saves, still delivers. Worship creates an atmosphere where He is not only welcomed, but also expected to show up—and when He shows up, things happen.

I try to encourage every church to teach their congregations biblical patterns of worship. These include Scriptures on praise and worship, physical expressions of praise and worship, the study of individuals and settings where worship is the central theme, worship in the priestly ministry under the Old Covenant, worship as seen through the types and shadows of the Jewish temple, the sacrificial system, blood covenant, Hebrew and Greek word studies—the list goes on and on. When people explore these areas, they will begin to properly understand that worship is a lifestyle, and that corporate worship is the most important thing we can do as the Body of Christ. As people are progressively being set free in their understanding of the Word when it deals with worship and why we worship, they will begin to experience God in a fresh new way. This, in turn, has a profound impact upon both our individual and corporate worship times.

Starting with the Basics

Enter His gates with thanksgiving
and His courts with praise.
Give thanks to Him and praise His name.
(Ps. 100:4)

We need to teach people some basic things. As basic as this: we enter His gates with thanksgiving. After we have gone through the gates properly, the courts of God can be accessed through the door of praise. And after the courts comes the Holy Place where we can enter in by the blood of

Jesus Christ to offer up ourselves as living sacrifices in worship to our God.

In general, people will be willing to move into new areas of praise and worship when they have been taught from the Word and then experienced it for themselves. People are afraid of what they don't know. When they come to know truth, the Holy Spirit will aid their understanding.

If you are ever going to move beyond where you are in worship, whether individually or corporately, you will have to take some risks. In order to get "there," you have to be willing to leave "here." In other words, you are going to have to trust God. We don't set the rules, He does. He does have just a bit to say about worship. We must listen.

As I experienced God in an exciting way through my university years, I saw and heard things in various places of worship that I had never heard in the church where I was raised. I couldn't understand how these people could be right in how they expressed their love to the Lord because I had never been taught that way. Slowly, God's Holy Spirit was teaching me that there were many ways to express my praise and worship to the Lord Jesus Christ. I had simply not been taught or exposed to these new ways of praising the Lord. They were not new to the church, but they were new to me. Many times, sadly, when something is not in our experience or tradition, we immediately dismiss it as an unacceptable expression of Christianity.

When I was a theology student, I spent some time visiting several churches in the area to see what all this "worship talk" was about. Some churches in the city were growing tremendously, and the primary reasons people gave for the growth had to do with their style of worship—their openness to God's presence in their services. My friends and fellow classmates had no idea that I was covertly visiting "enemy territory" (because we were not supposed to visit other denominations) on Sunday nights while serving on staff at my denominational church on Sunday morning.

I will never forget the first time I played hooky and visited one of "those other" churches that "didn't believe like we did." I hardly knew what to expect, so I arrived conveniently late so I could sit in the back. As I came through the doors of the sanctuary, the people were standing with their hands raised toward heaven, and the hair on the back of my neck stood up as I sensed God's presence touching me even before I had found a seat. I was overcome by God's presence, and I knew I was in the right place.

I had never seen people worship the way those people did. My first thought was, *This is what I have been looking for.* The songs were sung directly to God in the first person, and people wept and danced and bent low with their faces to the ground before an awesome God. People gave testimonies of His saving power in their lives. As I drove back to the dorm, I was awestruck. I knew that what I had tasted had ruined me—I was undone. That night started me on my way to discovering new depths in worshiping God.

A few weeks after I started attending my "Sunday Night Church," I was in the weekly chapel at the school and we were singing a song prior to prayer time. Without thinking, I raised both my hands to the Lord, as I was lost in the worship. It would have been OK if I had only raised one hand—but two hands meant I had obviously been visiting other churches. As soon as chapel was over, the local district superintendent's son came up to me and informed me that he was going to report me to his dad. When I asked why, he told me that he was looking around during prayer time and said, "I actually saw you with both hands up—and I'm reporting you. You're obviously one of *those* kinds of people!"

Of course, he would not have listened to me even if I had shown him the Scriptures where it says, "Lift your hands [plural] to the Lord" (Ps. 63:4; 119:48; 134:2). Even though it's funny to look back on it, it is also very sad because it illustrates how any one of us can become hardened and unteachable to new things in the Lord. Our relationship with the Lord should be dynamic, not static. God is a creative God, and Jesus promised us that the Holy Spirit would continue to reveal things to us as we daily walked with Him (John 14:26). Without a teachable spirit, we will learn nothing new from the Lord. I want to move on from milk to the meat of what God is saying and doing in me and in His church. God is always speaking—that is not the problem. The question is: am I listening?

> *We can never assume we know it all. We need to be lifelong students of the Word and of the Holy Spirit.*

We can never assume we know it all. We need to be lifelong students of the Word and of the Holy Spirit. We will never "arrive" until we go to be with Jesus. Too many times we have relied on yesterday's manna to nourish us today, tomorrow, and the rest of the week. God rebuked Israel for trying to stockpile the manna! He promised them that He would provide fresh food for them every day. God does have a way of getting His point across. When they went to the cupboard the next day to feed on the manna they had collected the day before—just in case God forgot to provide that day's needs—they found the manna rotten and full of maggots. They were not supposed to live off yesterday's visitation, yesterday's manifestation, yesterday's provision. God is big enough and powerful enough to provide something fresh every day of our lives. Don't be satisfied with what happened yesterday—God is doing something new and unique today!

One of the most important lessons about worship is that we must maintain open hearts and teachable spirits. We do not want to become professional worship connoisseurs, picking and choosing our way along, without taking any risks.

In order to learn and experience new depths and new heights in the worship of God, we must ask Him what it is that would please His heart. What does He want me to do today that would bring Him the most glory and honor? What would He want me to add to our worship service that would be fresh and innovative? Do we really think that God is so boring that we have to do things the same Sunday after Sunday, and worship service after worship service, year after year after year? I believe that the leading of the Holy Spirit is far more creative than that. God is not the one who gets in a rut—we are! Can you imagine the Holy Spirit telling the pastor or worship leader as they prepare for the next worship service, "Man, you guys are on your own. . . . Do what you want. . . . I'm fresh out of creativity today," or, "Well, if you can't think of anything else, just sing 'All Hail King Jesus.'"

Worship Is Not Just Words

It is important to understand that praise and worship are not only vocal but also audible and visible—all of which are scriptural.

My dear friend Greg Nelson told me once, "David, I don't go to church because I feel like it all the time or because I want to make someone happy. . . . I go because I owe Him! Because every time I ask for forgiveness, He forgives me. Every time I need Him, He's there. Every time I pray about something, He answers me. I owe Him. I go to church to worship because I owe Him a debt of gratitude!" He is exactly right—it's not about us, it's about Him. The most important thing we can do is tell God how much we love Him and express it in a multitude of ways. It warms His heart to hear you praise and thank Him. And don't think for a moment that He doesn't know when your voice is absent from among those offering up praise. Let me illustrate this with Scripture.

While traveling to Jerusalem, He passed between Samaria and Galilee. As He entered a village, 10 men with serious skin diseases met Him. They stood at a distance and raised their voices, saying, "Jesus, Master, have mercy on us!"

When He saw them, He told them, "Go and show yourselves to the priests." And while they were going, they were healed.

But one of them, seeing that he was healed, returned and, with a loud voice, gave glory to God. He fell facedown at His feet, thanking Him. And he was a Samaritan.

Then Jesus said, "Were not 10 cleansed? Where are the nine? Didn't any return to give glory to God except this foreigner?" And He told him, "Get up and go on your way. Your faith has made you well." (Luke 17:11–19)

Wow! Where do we begin to discuss all the lessons on worship contained in just these verses? What a picture of the church today. The Lord does so much for each one of us on a daily basis, yet how often do we remember to thank Him and praise Him? We have allowed ourselves to be lulled into some arrogant attitude that whispers to our hearts that we deserve His blessings—surely God doesn't expect us to thank Him for every little thing! Not only

> *God is not the one who gets in a rut—we are!*

is that attitude full of pride and sin, but it's a shame that so many of us experience the goodness and blessings of God on our lives and don't stop to render worship to His great Name. How this must grieve His heart!

Have you ever given someone a gift and that person never even acknowledged the gift or said, "Thanks"? It hurts, doesn't it? You still love and care for the person, but you think to yourself, *Why did I even bother?* You probably wouldn't ask for the gift back—you would just shrug your shoulders and go on.

> It is important to understand that praise and worship are not only vocal but also audible, and visible—all of which are scriptural.

Jesus did not take back the healing of the nine lepers when they refused to render praise for their healing—but He did question why only one returned to give Him thanks. Undoubtedly, this must have hurt the Master because He loved them all the same and gave them each the same gift of healing, yet only one fell at His feet in worship. And that one was doubly blessed that day! All ten had the opportunity to spend time with Jesus, but only one took advantage of it. All ten had the opportunity to have their sins forgiven, but only one put his faith in Jesus to be made well on the inside as well as the out.

The one who returned to worship was not "from the church"—he was a foreigner, an outcast, from the wrong side of town. Could it be that we in the church have become so proud and so full of ourselves that we have taken God's grace and power for granted? Who do we think we are? Have we looked down our noses at "worship novices" who still pray over their meals in public, who mention Jesus' name out loud in a crowd, who worship Him with an abandon that makes us uncomfortable? God forgive us!

You cannot tell me that God does not miss our praise. Jesus knew there were nine voices missing that day at the praise and worship service after the healing. Only one showed up, only one obeyed the prompting of his heart, and only one got to enjoy the presence of Jesus.

No one can thank Him for you—you have to do that for yourself. No one else can tell Him what is in your heart. There are no worship proxies. There is no such thing as a worship power of attorney. He knows what He has done for us and He knows whether or not we have returned to give Him thanks.

We are to "Enter His gates with thanksgiving. . . ." So many of us are not entering in because we have neglected to thank Him. How much richer and fuller would our relationship be if we worshiped at His feet daily? If we are in love with the Lord, shouldn't we be telling Him? We need to lift our hearts, hands, and voices to Him every day in loving adoration for all that He has done, is doing, and continues to do.

Worship should be the most important thing we do and should be our highest priority. Even in a corporate worship service, it is the worship that softens the hearts of those present to receive the seed of the Word of God. The Holy Spirit is drawing us closer and closer as we worship. The "Deep" in God (God's Holy Spirit) is calling unto the "deep" in us (Ps. 42:7). The Holy Spirit is working in many different ways in any given setting where Jesus Christ is being exalted. He is the ultimate Multitasker, pouring out the oil and wine and manifesting God's presence in our midst.

God reveals Himself in fresh ways as we worship. You will never understand worship by human philosophy or earthly wisdom. William Graham MacDonald wrote, "Philosophy depends on definitions for its constructions. Biblical theology, on the other hand, develops descriptions of what God does, and that divine dimension takes us beyond the outer limits of definitions, of human understanding, and of do-it-yourself formulas. Since the personal God cannot be known by definition but only as He reveals Himself, we must enter His temple worshiping in order to understand."[1]

Worship Is a Lifestyle

Worship is not just a time/space event. Though we have been talking a lot about a worship service, that time/space event should be simply an outflow, just one expression, of a lifestyle of worship. Worship is our highest priority.

Worship at its core is all about a relationship between God and His people. While I agree that unfortunately there will be church people singing songs to a God who they have no relationship with (lukewarm Christians), and there will always be people who incorrectly equate worship with just music, the larger picture tells us that this current worship movement is having a profound and positive effect upon the church and her mission.

When we enter into specific time/space events to worship, we should come expecting God to move. When we worship Him through the course of our days, we should expect God to move. He is the Author and Finisher of our faith, the Alpha and Omega, the Almighty One, the Redeemer, the Prince of Peace, the Anchor Behind the Veil, the Most High, the Bright and Morning Star, the Rose of Sharon, the Lily of the Valley, the Lamb of God, the Son of God, the Savior, the Counselor, the Everlasting Father, the Amen. When we understand that He is all that and more, shouldn't we expect something to happen when we worship Him? Shouldn't we expect Him to show up? Shouldn't we expect a response? The Scriptures and church history tell us the answer is a resounding "Yes!" Since God reveals Himself in worship, we must enter His temple worshiping in order to understand Him more fully.

What matters most is not where I worship, or even my body's posture, but the posture of my heart when I worship. Worship must be more than just rote and rites; it must become to every born-again believer—and every congregation—a living, dynamic, spiritual reality. God is spirit, and we are called in John 4:24 to worship Him in spirit and in truth. God is looking for more than converts—He's looking for converts who will worship Him in spirit and in truth.

"But an hour is coming, and *is now here,* when the true worshipers will worship the Father in spirit and truth. Yes, the Father wants such people to worship Him. God is spirit, and those who worship Him must worship in spirit and truth" (John 4:23–24, emphasis added). If the hour was *"now here"* when Jesus spoke these words two thousand years ago, certainly we're within that hour now! The world needs this hour when true worshipers will exalt His great name, and, as He is lifted up, the Holy Spirit will draw the hearts of millions to Him.

> *Worship at its core is all about a relationship between God and His people.*

The global emphasis on worship throughout the church of the Lord Jesus Christ is not by chance—nor is it a passing fad. We are within the hour when the world needs it. As the Lord gives us eyes to see and ears to hear, we are learning to worship from a foundation of truth that is continually setting us free in every dimension of our being. As that is taking place, we are moving into worshiping Him in the Spirit ("Deep calling unto deep"). So with our hearts and minds set on Him, we are experiencing things today in the realm of worship that are changing all our "presets."

God has raised up men and women throughout the history of the church who have given new life to worship styles and musical tastes along the way—that is not new. What is new is that we are seeing denominational worship styles—styles that once were unique to only certain segments of the church—amalgamated together as the Holy Spirit working in people's hearts is lowering barriers—barriers that have existed for centuries—in order to exalt the Lord Jesus

Christ! Thus, it is not uncommon to see evangelical churches using the Stations of the Cross as part of their worship, nor is it strange now to find liturgical congregations worshiping with upraised hands and worship bands. There are no presets anymore. And I think that's the way God wants it. As long as it's "in spirit and truth" and He is the One being lifted up and exalted, I believe His heart is warmed as His creativity is released in us through expressions of praise back to our Creator.

> As the Lord gives us eyes to see and ears to hear, we are learning to worship from a foundation of truth that is continually setting us free at every dimension of our being.

The Bible declares that "all the earth will worship You and sing praise to You" (Ps. 66:4). This very thing is taking place before our eyes. The current global interest in worship is a manifestation of this verse. People are hungering more than ever to experience God, and He is answering that hunger. The crescendo is getting louder and louder and attracting more and more attention from those who want to know this God we are so in love with—and who are finding out that He is wildly in love with them.

Worship is not a someday thing, or a one day thing.
It is, in fact, a right now, every day thing.

Chapter 2

Worship: A Two-Way Street

§ § §

*T*he praise and worship of God is an eternal activity that has no known beginning and will have no end. There are numerous references in God's Word that give us glimpses into the dateless past, as well as the future of, this awesome eternal activity.

One of these glimpses comes when God addresses Job:
Where were you when I established the earth?
Tell Me, if you have understanding.
Who fixed its dimensions?
Certainly you know!
Who stretched a measuring line across it?
What supports its foundations?
Or who laid its cornerstone
while the morning stars sang together
and all the sons of God shouted for joy? (Job 38:4–7)

When God was fashioning the heavens, planets, and galaxies, even His creation praised Him. "The morning stars sang" and His angels "shouted for joy" (Job 38:7)! I know that it's hard to explain all of this, let alone try to comprehend the enormity of what we are exploring, but even Jesus told us that creation has within it the ability to praise God all on its own. The Pharisees told Jesus to rebuke His disciples for openly praising God with loud voices for the miracles they had seen. Jesus answered, "I tell you, if they were to keep silent, the stones would cry out!" (See Luke 19:37–40.)

Throughout the Bible, all of creation stands as an eye-witness to God's actions and responds accordingly with praise and thankfulness.

> May the LORD God, the God of Israel, be praised,
> who alone does wonders.
> May His glorious name *be praised forever;*
> *the whole earth is filled with His glory.*
> Amen and amen. (Ps. 72:18–19, emphasis added)

> I heard *every creature in heaven, on earth, under*
> *the earth, on the sea, and everything in them say:*
>   Blessing and honor and glory and dominion
>   to the One seated on the throne,
>   and to the Lamb, forever and ever!
>   (Rev. 5:13, emphasis added).

Given just these two passages of Scripture alone, it is easy for us to conclude that if inanimate created objects will render praise, shouldn't mankind, the chief of His entire creation, offer up the same—even more?

Not only is the Lord to be "praised forever," but that praise is to emanate from everything and everyone. However, there is something altogether unique about the praise and worship that we as redeemed humans can bring to God.

The praise that we can offer is different from that of a tree, rock, animal, or even an angel. Ours is a personal praise, for only a human being can know what it is to be lost and then found. Only a human being can know what it is to be in sin and be forgiven. Only a human being can know the feeling that comes from being born again, being filled with God's Holy Spirit, being set free from oppression, being healed, being delivered. Every time we tell the Lord how much we love Him, we are reminding Him that the gift of His dear Son Jesus was worth it. He craved a relationship with us so much that He willingly gave up His only Son to die for our sins, so that what was lost in the Garden of Eden might be restored through the shedding of His precious blood.

> *Ours is a personal praise, for only a human being can know what it is to be lost and then found.*

Even John's revelation reveals to us that praise and worship go on continually in heaven and will never cease. Many times as I have read through Revelation 4 and 5, I have been exhausted as I try to comprehend the scene. I encourage you to get your Bible and read through those chapters. There are so many things I could mention, but I will share just a few:

Each of the four living creatures had six wings; they were covered with eyes around and inside. *Day and night they never stop, saying*:

Holy, holy, holy,
Lord God, the Almighty,
who was, who is, and who is coming.

Whenever the living creatures give glory, honor, and thanks to the One seated on the throne, the One who lives forever and ever, *the 24 elders fall down before the One seated on the throne, worship the One who lives forever and ever, cast their crowns before the throne, and say*:

Our Lord and God,
You are worthy to receive
glory and honor and power,
because You have created all things,

and because of Your will
they exist and were created. (Rev. 4:8–11)

Did you notice in verse 8, "Day and night they never stop, saying . . ."? If the living creatures "never stop," then the twenty-four elders don't either because it says that every time the living creatures give glory, honor, and thanks, the elders fall down before the throne of God in worship and say, "Our Lord and God, You are worthy. . . ."

When we enter into worship, we are engaging in something that is already going on in glory. Imagine what this symphony of praise and worship must sound like to our Lord! The millions upon millions of angels who are singing, the living creatures, the seraphim, the cherubim, the twenty-four elders, the saints who are already in heaven and the redeemed that are still on the earth—*wow!*

Time to Worship

Worship is both an eternal thing and a right now, every day thing! Though there may be time-space events where we come together specifically to worship God with other believers, we must remember that there is a worship service already going on that is not bound to any time-space event—it is eternal. If praise and worship are not important, why do they dominate so much of God's Word? If praise and worship are not close to God's heart, then why is it going on all the time around His throne? He could stop it if He wanted to, but He doesn't.

Anytime is a good time to worship the Lord. Whether you are at home, on the job, driving down the road (as long as you're careful), or in the shower, go ahead and tell the Lord how much you love Him and what He means to you. The point is, worship is not just for Sundays at 10:30 a.m.—it happens whenever you reach out to God in loving surrender and open your heart up to Him. Worship happens when our hearts respond to God's heart. Worship happens when we pour out our souls to Him. Worship happens when we make it abundantly clear to Him that we know we cannot make it on our own—we need Him!

As we begin to tap into that which is already going on, our worship *to* God becomes an avenue of spiritual resource *from* God. Both Scripture and experience have taught the church that when she worships, a divine ebb and flow begins to

> *When we enter into worship, we are engaging in something that is already going on in glory.*

take place as God hears and receives from His children and His children hear and receive from Him. As praise and worship go up, His weighty presence—His glory—descends. God receives and responds.

Worship is fluid, dynamic, and unpredictable—because life is. We respond to God as we process the highs and lows of life on a daily basis. Worship becomes the catalyst whereby God manifests Himself in the midst of His people. We will explore this more thoroughly later, but I want you to know that when we praise and worship God, we invoke His presence! When we worship God, we are enthroning Him in our praises. We are spiritually creating a throne where He can come and sit down in our midst and enjoy the praises of His children. Praise is God's permanent address. Praise is where He is found. Praise is the atmosphere of heaven. When we praise and worship the Lord, not only is He blessed, but we are strengthened in the process as His Spirit whispers courage to our hearts, peace to our minds, and healing to our souls.

A Unique Worship Experience

We all have different experiences when it comes to God's holy presence. The continuing challenge for all of us will be to not build a shrine to those experiences and somehow think that's all there is. We cannot camp out on some past experience and have a fresh worship encounter with God. He will be off down the road somewhere, and we will be hanging back guarding some empty room of what used to be.

> *Worship is fluid, dynamic, and unpredictable— because life is. We respond to God as we process the highs and lows of life on a daily basis.*

A young bride wanted to impress her husband and all the family by cooking their first Thanksgiving meal. She took a huge turkey, stuffed it, and then, much to the disbelief of her husband, chopped it in two. She put one half in their big, brand-new oven and threw the other half away.

He asked her, "Why did you do that?"

She replied, "My family has always done it that way. My mom and my grandmother always chopped the turkey in two, threw half away, and put the other half in the oven." The husband was puzzled.

Once all the families had arrived, he insisted that she ask her mother why they had always chopped the turkey in two before putting it in the oven. Her mom didn't know, so she turned to Grandma. "Grandma, why do we always chop the turkey in two and throw half of it out before we put it in the oven?"

Grandma matter-of-factly replied, "Because our oven wasn't big enough."

Doesn't that sound like a lot of church arguments? "Well, we've always done it that way, and we're not going to start doing things different now." "We've been singing those songs for two hundred years, and we're not learning new ones now." "God loves the pipe organ." "Oh, we can't have *him* lead worship—we'll lose people." "We only celebrate Communion twice a year—we always have."

I have heard hundreds of arguments and discussions about

praise and worship and what is the "appropriate, accepted, and informed" response we should all have to God's presence. Don't buy into that! Where do you think the supposed "appropriate, accepted, and informed" responses come from? Someone or some church's experience that has been passed down from generation to generation. Aren't you tired of that kind of thinking?

> *This world is hungry for the presence of God.*

Who do we think we are? Could it be that the reason many churches are empty is that we have been standing guard over some stale experience that someone had years ago?

People coming into our churches don't care whose name is on the brass plate at the end of the pew. They are hungry for an experience—an encounter—with Almighty God. And if they can't find it in church, they'll go where they can! This world is hungry for the presence of God. People need to know that they can experience it not only in church, but in their everyday lives as well. In fact, if people are encountering God every day, it will make what happens in our churches explosive. Of course we have our personal tastes, but we can't let them get in the way of allowing the Holy Spirit to lead us into the depths of experiencing the Lord's presence.

Worship is a two-way street: it is giving and receiving. God designed it so that we can draw near to Him and He in turn will draw near to us (see James 4:8). And when God draws near, He speaks, leads, directs, empowers, heals, and moves in us.

Ordained to Praise

O Lord, our Lord,
how majestic is your name in all the earth!
You have set your glory above the heavens.
From the lips of children and infants

you have ordained praise because of your enemies,
to silence the foe and the avenger. (Ps. 8:1–2 NIV)

Praise and worship are part of our spiritual DNA. We
were created with the capacity to praise, worship, and
honor God. From the lips of children and infants, God
has ordained praise because it stops the enemy dead in his
tracks! What an awesome truth. The Hebrew word used
for "praise" is *oze*, which can also be translated "strength."
Isn't that great? Praise and strength can be used inter-
changeably. When we praise God, He gives us strength for
the battle; we draw strength from our times of praise and
worship to the Lord!

From the lips of children and infants, God has established or ordained praise because it has a paralyzing affect
upon His (and our) enemies. Neither the devil nor his
demons can offer any kind of protest after praise. They are
silenced. Clearly the praise of the Most High God silences
the enemy. The word *silence* in Psalm 8:2 means to cause
to fall, to depose, to cause to suffer or to be lacking, to put
down, and to take away!

In heaven, praise is a continuing exercise; it always has
been and always will be. It is forever etched into the memories of Satan and his demons. If anyone knew the power,
majesty, and fulfillment of praise and worship, it would have
been them. Yet they assumed that they were more important
than God and became full of themselves and fell—literally—
from their sacred positions.

When God's people lift up His praise and worship their
King, our heartfelt expressions must strike panic and fear
into the enemy camp. How our praise of the Holy must
remind them of their futile attempt to ascend above the
Lord! For all eternity, they will have to exist with the irritat-
ing sound of the redeemed praising and worshiping the Lord

they so foolishly challenged. Even hell cannot escape the sound of His praise, for one day soon,

> At the name of Jesus every knee [will] bow—
> of those who are in heaven and on earth
> and under the earth—
> and every tongue confess that Jesus Christ is Lord,
> to the glory of God the Father. (Phil. 2:10–11)

There is a throne—an occupied throne—and that throne is at the center of our vast universe. It is the center of all that was, and is, and is to come. Upon that great throne sits the Almighty Jehovah God, the God of Abraham, Isaac, and Jacob. He is our God as well. His Word at some point reached our ears and touched our lives and made them different. It was at that moment that He breathed

> *If He knew us before we were born, then surely there is something about us that recognizes the presence of the Lord when we encounter it!*

the breath of life into us, as we were born again. Instantly, it became natural for us to praise Him who sits upon the throne. It became natural for each of us to lift up a sacrifice of praise for all that He had done, was doing, and has promised to do.

Jesus quoted this passage when He was cleansing the temple and the children were praising him:

> When the chief priests and the scribes saw the wonders that He did and the children in the temple complex cheering, "*Hosanna* to the Son of David!" they were indignant and said to Him, "Do you hear what these children are saying?"
> "Yes," Jesus told them. "Have you never read:
> 'You have prepared praise from the mouths of children and nursing infants?'"
> (Matt. 21:15–16)

How do children know to praise Him? How were those children able to recognize that He was the Son of David when many adults refused to say so? Because praise and worship form a part of our spiritual DNA! It's there before we are born. Can you imagine what Jesus must have felt as these little kids loved on Him through their words of worship? If He knew us before we were born, then surely there is something about us that recognizes the presence of the Lord when we encounter it! He made us, He knows us best, and He knit us together!

Remember when Elizabeth, the mother of John the Baptist, received a visit from Mary? When Mary entered the room, the baby within Elizabeth (who would grow up to be John the Baptist) leaped for joy inside her (Luke 1:44). How is that possible? Again, because praise and worship form a part of our spiritual DNA. God has ordained it.

You and I are worshiping something or someone all the time. Everyone in this world is worshiping something—but for most people, it's not God. We are all worshipers—we're just not all worshiping the same thing. In a similar way, our giftings, talents, abilities, and so forth, come from the same God, but not everyone uses those things to glorify Him.

Worship is quite simply a relationship between God and His people. Using Scripture, we have begun to open the envelope of why worship is our highest priority. Our God has ordained us to praise and worship Him and He in turn inhabits our praise. As we worship Him, His heart is moved to communicate back to us.

Worship is a two-way street. Let's not cheat God of the opportunity to speak into our times with Him. Let's not just praise Him and get on with the day . . . let's praise Him and then listen! You were made for this. Go ahead and tap into what's already going on. He is waiting to hear your voice and longs for you to hear His.

Chapter 3

Worship: Hungering for God's Presence

§ § §

*I*f you could ask God for anything, what would it be? Where you are in life might have something to do with what you would ask for. Would you ask for money, a car, a new job, a new house, or other material things? Or, would you ask for health, food, clothes, and enough to get by?

If you could ask God for anything, what would it be? It's an interesting question and our answers tell a lot about where we are in our walk with God. What we ask for from God says a lot about ourselves. Did you ever think of that?

When we are newly born again in Christ Jesus, just like a young baby or toddler who has just learned to speak, we act pretty much the same. We have yet to understand that God is going to take care of all of our needs, watch over us, lead us, guide us, and protect us. We see it in His Word, but it hasn't sunk from our heads into our hearts yet. So as baby Christians we pray things like "Jesus, bless me. Jesus, feed me. Jesus, give me. Jesus, I want. Jesus, I need. Jesus, do this. Jesus, do that." We don't yet pray on a higher level. We don't think beyond our own needs.

My own young children used to ask for a drink of water, or a bite of something to eat, or "Dad, can you reach this?" or "Dad, can you reach that for me?" Now they have learned to get their own drinks, open the pantry door and get their own snacks, climb up on the counter and get their own cups. They have learned that Mom and Dad always make sure that there is something in the pantry and something in the refrigerator. They don't have to worry about shopping for groceries. They know that Mom and Dad will supply their needs and that they have free access to whatever's on the shelves at home. Now they ask for money or a car or permission to stay out until midnight!

After awhile, hopefully, we reach the point in our relationship with God where we understand that He has promised to meet our needs according to His glorious riches, and that while we give thanks always for those necessities, we don't have to go to Him daily to ask for them. He has promised we would have them and that He would daily supply our needs. Thus, we move on in our prayer lives and begin to pray about other things. We come to the place where we realize that there is a whole lot more to God than just asking Him to bless us. We come to understand that He is more than a big vending machine or some divine charity organization. *If you could ask God for anything, what would it be?*

Show Me Your Way

One man believed on God for his deliverance, and God saved him. The man soon discovered that God supplied him and all of his people with food and water every day. God made sure to meet their needs, just as He had promised to do. But there came a time when this man understood at a deeper level that God was serious when He said He'd meet their needs. That truth had dropped from his head to his heart. Now he had a hunger for more spiritual things. His prayer life began to change.

In Exodus 33:7–23, Moses meets with God and has the opportunity to ask Him for anything in the universe. I think God would have given him anything he wanted. Moses didn't ask for more food. He didn't ask for gold or silver, prestige or riches. No, Moses had a desire for something far deeper, something higher, something beyond himself, something eternal, something spiritual. Moses had just two requests: "Show me Your way," and "Show me Your glory."

"Now therefore, I pray, if I have found grace in Your sight, show me now Your way, that I may know You and that I may find grace in Your sight" (Exod. 33:13 NKJV). "Please, show me Your glory" (Exod. 33:18 NKJV). Wow! Moses could have asked for anything—and he did. "Show me Your way" and "show me Your glory."

What does this tell us about Moses' heart? Jesus told us, "For the mouth speaks from the overflow of the heart" (Matt. 12:34). Moses' two prayer requests poured forth so easily because they had been stored up in his heart. This is what he was longing for. This is what he had been waiting to see. This is what he must have dreamed about for so long. He must have thought, *If I ever get the chance, . . . if God ever asks me, . . . if God should allow me the privilege to request something, I know what I want.*

Of course, God already knew what Moses was going to ask. You see, God sees our hearts and God certainly knew what was in Moses' heart that day. God knew his motives were pure—they were not out of some selfish lust for gain or prideful egocentricity. Moses was motivated by his love for Jehovah and his personal desire to know in as intimate detail as possible this God of Israel. Moses both loved and feared God, but he trusted in His mercy enough to make his requests known. He must have thought, *Well, if I'm going to ask, I might as well do it now. If I offend Him, He knows I'm not trying to. I have no interest in anything else. I want to know Him at any cost.* Moses hungered for God's holy presence!

The Amplified Bible puts it this way: "Now therefore, I pray You, if I have found favor in Your sight, show me now Your way, that I may know You [progressively become more deeply and intimately acquainted with You, perceiving and recognizing and understanding more strongly and clearly] and that I may find favor in Your sight" (Exod. 33:13).

When Moses said, "Show me now Your way," he wasn't saying, "Point me in the right direction and I'll take it from here." He was saying, "Show me the course of life and how You'd have me live it." He was saying, "Show me and walk with me in the journey." Moses wasn't interested in God's ways just because he desired information. His desire came from a heart of a worshiper that was saying, "I want to sign up with You for life—not just a chapter of it. I want to walk into eternity with You."

In his prayer, we see the reasons why Moses asked, "Show me now Your way." He gave us two distinct reasons for his request: "that I may know You" and "that I may find grace [favor] in Your sight."

Knowing God

When we say we know someone, what exactly does that mean? When I am talking about knowing someone I have just met, is it the same as knowing a friend for years? When I say I have known this particular friend for years, is it the same as the way I know my wife? When someone says she knows how to operate a computer, does she mean she knows how to compile source code or just how to turn it on and run a few applications? When I look up into the heavens and see the stars, I say to myself, *I know those are stars up there, but beyond naming a few, I don't know anything about them.* "Knowing" someone or something has varying degrees—it's a relative term.

Conversely, have you ever known someone who did something just terrible and shocking, and you saw him on the evening news or read about him in the paper? You said to yourself, *You think you know someone, and then....*" Or, have you ever had a time when you discovered something, maybe in your line of work, that you had never learned before? Even with all your training and education, you discover something, and you say, "Wow, you learn something new every day!" That is an example of progressive knowledge.

A true expert in any field of study, whether it is medicine, agriculture, anthropology, industry, computers, or even theology, understands that you never "arrive." You are always learning new things. If you are going to master a subject, you must be committed to being a lifelong student of your subject.

The verb *to know* has several definitions. It can mean:
- To perceive directly, grasp in the mind with clarity or certainty.
- To have a practical understanding of, as through experience; be skilled in: *He knows how to cook.*
- To perceive as familiar; recognize: *I know that face.*
- To be acquainted with: *He doesn't know his neighbors.*
- To be able to distinguish; recognize as distinct: *She knows right from wrong.*

When Moses said, "Show me now Your way, that I may know You," what did he mean? He meant that he wanted to become progressively more intimately acquainted with the living God. He was saying, "I want to experience You every day of my life! I don't want to know just facts about You—I want to know You in all of Your glory!" He was talking about a *relationship!*

God wants a relationship with you and me. That is why He told Moses His presence would go with Him and the children of Israel—because He longed to be in relationship with His people. Even if He had to love them through a veil, He still wanted a relationship. Even if He had to love them through the smoke screen of burning animal flesh, He still wanted a relationship. Even if He had to love them by way of sacrificial blood being applied to the mercy seat, He still wanted a relationship. It has always been about relationship. It has always been about experiencing life every day with His people. It has always been about loving you. You didn't choose Him, He chose you!

> *God is totally in love with you and desperately wants to have a relationship with you where you can know Him.*

That is why He met His people in the tabernacle, why He brought them out of Egypt and guided them with a pillar of fire and a cloud. He wanted a relationship. That is why He manifests Himself in the praises of His people and answers their prayers. That is why all you have to do is breathe His name and He will show up. It's about relationship. God is totally in love with you and desperately wants to have a relationship with you where you can know Him.

Both the Old and New Testaments prove that you can worship a God you don't know. You can even experience a measure of God's grace in your life and still not know Him. You can know (have an understanding) that Jesus died for your sins. You can know that He will save you if you repent, believe, and confess Him as Savior. You can know facts and figures, dates and times, and still not really know the One who loved you first. *What a shame it would be to be saved and not really enter into the joy of knowing Him!* Sadly, people do it all the time. Our churches are full of people who know who He is but don't really know Him as He wants to be known.

Drawing Near to God

In order to know God, you will need to put forth some effort. But if you love Him, it won't seem like any effort at all. When you met your spouse, did it seem like effort to get to know him or her? When you became friends with someone you really liked and found that you had a lot in common, did it seem like an effort to get to know that person? Of course not. When you fall in love with God, you want to know everything about Him. You could live a million lifetimes, and there would still be more you would like to learn about God.

One of the keys to getting to know God is at the heart of Moses' prayer: hunger. Moses hungered for God. Moses longed for God. Moses realized that nothing else in the world could compare to the experience of being with God. Moses had a passion for His presence. Moses had lost his appetite for other people and other things. He was hungry for God. And guess what? God will always answer that kind of prayer.

It was James, the brother of Jesus, who wrote to the believers in Jerusalem, "Draw near to God, and He will draw near to you. Cleanse your hands, sinners, and purify your hearts, double-minded people!" (James 4:8). If we draw near to God, He will reciprocate and draw near to us. Drawing near to God is spending time with Him, worshiping Him, praying and talking to Him, inviting Him into every aspect of our lives.

James then gives us the formula for drawing near. If you've committed sin, confess it, get rid of it, and put it under the blood of Jesus (in other words, keep a short sin account). Next, ask the Lord to examine your heart, your motives, and the things that make you do what you do. Bring your heart under His lordship as well. May our actions be manifestations of a clean heart and conscience.

Notice that when James writes about this he says, "Purify your hearts, double-minded people!" What does he mean by "double-minded"? A person who is double-minded is drawn in two completely different directions. Thus, he will get nowhere fast because his loyalty is divided and he vacillates between faith and unbelief. A double-minded person is unstable in all her ways and her spiritual walk is inconsistent because she tries to serve God and her own interests at the same time. We've all learned that this kind of living never works. You cannot serve two masters.

> *Our churches are full of people who know who He is but don't really know Him like He wants to be known.*

I learned a long time ago that I am not going to get very far with God by playing spiritual games. God doesn't play games! I soon discovered that the only people playing the game were me, myself, and I. It's just like people thinking that they can "ride the fence" into the kingdom. There is no riding the fence, there is no lukewarm support group—you're either in or out. If I really want to know Him, I'm going to have to get serious about my relationship with Him.

God our Father sent His Son, Jesus, in order that we might know Him more fully. Jesus was Emmanuel, God with us, God in the flesh, and God incarnate. God was willing to love us through a veil for awhile, but when the time was right, Jesus came and ripped the veil in two. He opened up a new and living way. He opened up permanent and perpetual access to God the Father by shedding His blood once and for all. His blood paved the way to restore God's relationship with you and me. Praise the Lord!

God loved the world so much that He gave His one and only Son so that whoever believes in Him will never perish but enjoy an eternal relationship with Him. Again, it's all about relationship. It has always been about relationship. From the moment Adam and Eve sinned in the Garden of Eden, God sought to reestablish relationship with His children. We couldn't get to where He was, so He came to us through Jesus. Until that time He loved us from afar, through or from behind a veil because sin cannot exist in the same place as God's glory.

But Jesus came and tore the veil so that we can get close to God. Now, when Father God looks at us, He looks at us through the blood of His Son, Jesus. Why wouldn't we want to know the height and depth and width of the One who came to redeem us? Why wouldn't we want to walk with Him and share our hearts' concerns? Why wouldn't we want to live to please the One who sought to restore our broken relationship?

> But everything that was a gain to me, I have considered to be a loss because of Christ. More than that, *I also consider everything to be a loss in view of the surpassing value of knowing Christ Jesus my Lord.* Because of Him I have suffered the loss of all things and consider them filth, so that I may gain Christ and be found in Him, not having a righteousness of my own from the law, but one that is through faith in Christ—the righteousness from God based on faith. *[My goal] is to know Him* and the power of His resurrection and the fellowship of His sufferings, being conformed to His death, assuming that I will somehow reach the resurrection from among the dead. (Phil. 3:7–11, emphasis added)

Paul is talking about a relationship here. This isn't "knowing" about the facts and figures of Jesus' life. Paul is pouring out his heart. Paul is hungering for God's presence.

Like Moses, he wants to know the Lord in a personal and experiential way. He wants his personal fellowship with Jesus to be more intimate, nearer still, even beyond what he had known up to that moment.

To really know Jesus personally and to understand His nature, His character, and His ways will require us to draw near to Him. We draw near by listening to His Word, following the leading of His Holy Spirit, responding positively to His dealings with us when it comes to spiritual matters, as well as carrying on the cause of His great gospel. If I want to know the power of His resurrection, then I must experience the renewal of my own life by being born again, and be set free from the bondage of sin. I must yield to the power of the Holy Spirit in order that I might be an effective witness for Christ Jesus. As a result, I will have a physical resurrection, when this mortal body will put on immortality and I will live with the Lord forever and ever.

"My goal is to know Him and the power of His resurrection and the fellowship of His sufferings, being conformed to His death." If I am to know Jesus and be a follower of Jesus, I must embrace His sufferings and His death. How? By daily picking up my personal cross and following Him. "Summoning the crowd along with His disciples, He said to them, 'If anyone wants to be My follower, he must deny himself, take up his cross, and follow Me. For whoever wants to save his life will lose it, but whoever loses his life because of Me and the gospel will save it'" (Mark 8:34–35).

We need that cross to kill our impure ways, our bad attitudes, our wrong motives, our ungodly thoughts, and daily remember the price that Jesus paid for our sins. We need that cross because something inside of us must die. Only God can resurrect us into a new life. We only need to wait and *know* that He is God.

Walking in God's Favor

Moses' second reason for asking God to "show me now Your way" is "that I may find grace in Your sight." The word *grace* can also be interchanged with the word *favor* because both English words come from the same Hebrew word definition. What exactly is the favor of God?

The Hebrew word used here for "grace" is *chen*. The idea of the word is "to stoop in kindness to an inferior and to have pity." It can have the idea of favor, graciousness, kindness, beauty, pleasantness, charm, attractiveness, loveliness, or affectionate regard. The root, *chanan*, means "to act graciously or mercifully toward someone; to be compassionate, and to be favorably inclined."

Moses is praying for the Lord to reveal to him His ways in order that he might walk and live within God's grace. When we walk within the perimeters of God's ways, which are the moral and spiritual framework or patterns for living revealed to us through His Word and through the example of His Son, Jesus Christ, we will find ourselves experiencing the favor of God.

Let's look at some verses in Scripture that confirm this:
For You, LORD, bless the righteous one;
You surround him with favor like a shield. (Ps. 5:12)

For His anger lasts only a moment,
but His favor, a lifetime.
Weeping may spend the night,
but there is joy in the morning. (Ps. 30:5)

For the LORD God is a sun and shield.
The LORD gives grace and glory;
He does not withhold the good
from those who live with integrity. (Ps. 84:11)

From these verses we see that as a result of our following the Lord, His favor will rest upon our lives. It is not something we earn from Him; it simply flows from the goodness of His heart toward us. You cannot earn God's grace. You cannot buy God's grace. You cannot work for God's grace. God's grace is a gift—that is why divine grace is described as "God's unmerited favor." We can do nothing in and of ourselves to merit such favor. It is bestowed upon us by His choosing.

> *Jesus was and is God meeting us at the point of our need.*

Moses could only experience a certain measure of God's grace and favor. The children of Israel still needed to sacrifice animals and apply the blood to the mercy seat within the Holy of Holies in order to continually and annually satisfy God's righteous requirements. In fact, all of those who lived righteous lives prior to the cross of Christ experienced God's grace and favor to a degree. But those who believe on the Lord Jesus can receive the total embodiment of God's grace and favor. Jesus was and is God meeting us at the point of our need.

God gave the law through Moses to reveal sin, but He graced mankind with His Son, Jesus, in order to deal with the sin problem on our behalf, once and for all. "For although the law was given through Moses; grace and truth came through Jesus Christ" (John 1:17). "The law came along to multiply the trespass. But where sin multiplied, grace multiplied even more, so that, just as sin reigned in death, so also grace will reign through righteousness, resulting in eternal life through Jesus Christ our Lord" (Rom. 5:20–21).

Jesus Christ not only fulfills God's promise of grace and favor, but He is grace and favor personified. The word for "grace" used here in these New Testament verses is *charis*, which means "graciousness of manner or act, undeserved blessing, unmerited favor, a free gift."

Everything that Jesus is about and everything that He has done and does for us individually and corporately is an act of graciousness. Furthermore, as born-again believers, we have the continual abiding of God's Holy Spirit dwelling within, influencing our hearts daily. What grace! What favor! People who hunger for God's presence will experience and come to know the ways of the Lord; for He will reveal them, and they will come to know the favor of the Lord upon their lives. His Holy Spirit within will continue to create the hunger within us for more and more of Him.

> *Our getting to know Him is not only our privilege and pleasure, but it is a holy journey that will last beyond this lifetime!*

Jesus speaks to us even as He did to the apostle Paul and says, "My grace is sufficient for you, for power is perfected in weakness" (2 Cor. 12:9). Jesus is saying to us today, "Live in Me, walk in Me, follow Me, acknowledge Me in all your ways, and I will make sure that the blessing on your life will never run out, the favor that I speak over your life will go on forever, and there will never be a time in which I will not supply exactly what you need exactly when you need it!"

When we come to the Lord in worship, we are saying, "God, I love you and I want to know You. I want to know Your ways and I want Your favor to rest upon everything in my life. I want to see Your glory!" If we weren't interested in these things, we wouldn't bother worshiping Him. The pouring out of our hearts in worship is essentially saying these things. We want to be with Him, and the more time we spend with Him, the more we get to know about Him. He already knows us—no one knows us better. Our getting to know Him is not only our privilege and pleasure, but it is a holy journey that will last beyond this lifetime. God's Spirit daily points the way and reminds us that we were made for this.

God's Presence:
The Distinguishing Factor

Before God ever showed Moses His glory, Moses had proven himself as a man hungry for God's presence. Moses was a worshiper and a man of prayer. Before God ever agreed to make all of His goodness pass by Moses, Moses had already shown that he was willing to persevere in prayer and worship God until the desired answer came. I think the same is true today. God is not going to reveal to us one thing until He sees that we are hungry for His presence, persevering in prayer, and willing to go the distance for others. God will reveal Himself to those He knows are serious about their relationship with Him.

Jesus told us that those who are hungry and thirst after righteousness will be filled. If we do not hunger and thirst after the things of God, then we won't be filled with those things—we will be lacking. Moses got what he asked for because he was serious about loving, worshiping, and serving God. He hungered after God's presence, he longed for God's ways, and he wanted to see God's glory. Moses was an imperfect human being like you and me. What God did for him He will do for us—but we must be driven by that hunger and thirst for more of the Lord!

And the Lord said, My Presence shall go with you, and I will give you rest.

And Moses said to the Lord, *If Your Presence does not go with me, do not carry us up from here!*

For by what shall it be known that I and Your people have found favor in Your sight? *Is it not in Your going with us so that we are distinguished, I and Your people, from all the other people upon the face of the earth?* (Exod. 33:14–16 AMP, emphasis added)

The Hebrew word for "Presence," *pâneh*, means "face." So what Moses is saying in the light of this definition is "If Your Presence [face] does not go with us, do not bring us up from here." Thus, the reason that "Presence" is capitalized here is that it specifically means Him, His face, His countenance, His appearance, His real, palpable, physical *presence.* Furthermore, to dwell in and live in God's presence means that there is a relationship present—you know each other face-to-face, you communicate, you are familiar, and yet He is God. His presence transforms, energizes, encourages, sets free, envelops, touches, heals, delivers, sanctifies, and fills. Everything that He does, everything that He's about, everything that He is, is all found in His presence. God's presence is the distinguishing factor among His people—His real people. The people who truly love, honor, and obey God will live, move, and have their being in His presence. God's presence does not abide with those who have not accepted Jesus Christ as their Savior. God's presence does not attend to the lives of those who reject His existence or deny that He alone is God and worthy of praise. His presence is what sets His people aside from all the peoples of the earth.

> *God's presence is the distinguishing factor among His people—His real people.*

God's presence does not rest on those who worship Muhammad, Buddha, Confucius, Mary Baker Eddy, L. Ron Hubbard, Jehovah's Witnesses, Latter Day Saints and Joseph Smith, Baha'i, astrology, palm reading, tarot card reading, Wicca, dead saints, dead people, dead things—God's presence will only reside within and upon those who have come to Him in faith through the blood of Jesus Christ, His only Son. There is no other God and there is no other way for mankind to be saved.

"Surely the righteous will praise Your name; the upright will live in Your presence" (Ps. 140:13). Do you give Him praise? Are you actively giving Him praise? He's counting on it. Out of all the people in the world, out of all the people who say they know Him, surely the righteous, the redeemed, the saved, the born again, are not ashamed to stand up and praise Him!

You can't be saved and have a problem with praise and worship. You can't be delivered and be uncomfortable with offering up thanks to His great name. Don't say you've had an encounter with God but it's a private thing. If you are really in love with Jesus, you are not going to care who knows. If you are really in a relationship with Jesus, it's going to show—because His presence in and on your life will be the distinguishing factor.

This verse tells us that "the upright will live in Your presence." We cannot be upright in and of ourselves. We are upright in Christ Jesus. He holds us up. Sometimes you think you're going to fall or faint, but Jesus comes and holds you up. He's constantly interceding for you, praying for you, lifting you up by and through His prayers and the indwelling presence of His Holy Spirit. The upright are those whose sins have been forgiven, who have accepted Jesus Christ as their personal Lord and Savior and are living and walking in the light of His will and Word. This is a great promise—the upright shall dwell in God's presence.

The same presence that brings us comfort and life will bring judgment, fear, and death to those who reject Him. Furthermore, when you are not living right, the first thing the enemy will encourage you to do is try to hide from the presence of God. However, nothing is hidden from God. He knows all, sees all, and is present everywhere. You cannot fool God. You are only fooling yourself if you think you can keep something from Him. Adam and Eve certainly found that out the hard way (see Gen. 3:8–10).

Sin will make you want to run and hide from God's presence. God's glory and sin cannot abide together. The Bible records what will happen in the last days. "And they [the people] said to the mountains and to the rocks, 'Fall on us and hide us from the face of the One seated on the throne and from the wrath of the Lamb, because the great day of Their wrath has come! And who is able to stand?'" (Rev. 6:16–17).

The importance of Jesus' sacrificial death on the cross is that He provided forgiveness and atonement for our sin so we can live and dwell in God's presence. Only the blood of Jesus can make you ready for God's presence. Jesus became the physical face of God to this lost and dying world. God's people can rely upon God's presence.

Even Creation recognizes God's presence: no person or thing can escape its reality.

The earth shook;
The heavens also dropped rain at the presence of God;
Sinai itself was moved at the presence of God,
   the God of Israel. (Ps. 68:8 NKJV)

His lightning lights up the world;
the earth sees and trembles.
The mountains melt like wax
at the presence of the LORD—
at the presence of the Lord of all the earth.
The heavens proclaim His righteousness;
all the peoples see His glory. (Ps. 97:4–6)

Though these verses from Psalms were written hundreds of years later, both Moses and David knew the same God and the same presence. It is no wonder that Moses prayed,

"If Your Presence does not go with me, do not carry us up from here." He knew that the presence of God equaled victory. He knew that the presence of God meant that everything they would ever need would be made available to them. He knew that without God's presence they might as well die in the desert.

Read these promises from God's Word about His presence, keeping in mind that the word *presence* can be rendered *face.*

When my enemies turn back,
they shall fall and perish at Your presence.
(Ps. 9:3 NKJV)

You reveal the path of life to me;
in Your presence is abundant joy;
in Your right hand are eternal pleasures. (Ps. 16:11)

Do not banish me from Your presence
or take Your Holy Spirit from me. (Ps. 51:11)

Where can I go to escape Your Spirit?
Where can I flee from Your presence? (Ps. 139:7)

These are just a few verses of the many that deal with the presence of God. Why would we ever want to do anything void of His presence? There would be no point. If God's presence doesn't go with us, if God's presence doesn't reside in us, if God's presence doesn't rest on our lives, then quite frankly there's no sense in living. It is His presence that brings life and fullness of joy and victory over our enemies. It is His presence that we must treasure, respect, honor, cherish, and hunger for. Once you've tasted God's presence, nothing else will satisfy.

Show Me Your Glory

Moses' other request was, "Please, show me Your glory" (Exod. 33:18 NKJV). Although we'll talk about God's glory in greater detail later, it's important for us to understand what Moses was talking about when he said, "Your glory." The Hebrew word for "glory" is *chabod*, which means "God's honor, renown, majesty, copiousness, weight, and His visible splendor." There's a word picture! God's glory is His visible splendor, which can come in many forms and manifestations. The word *glory* used in this setting is closely related to *presence* and *face*.

What a hunger Moses had. After all he had experienced with God, he still hungered for more. Would we have been content long before this, or would we have been driven by an even deeper insatiable hunger for more of God? Moses knew there was more where all the rest had come from. Now he wanted to see God's raw essence without a veil over his eyes. Of course, God granted to Moses only what he could take because Moses was a man and no man can see the face of God and live to tell about it on this side of heaven. God knew that even a glimpse of His glory passing by would so transform Moses that he would never be the same. Our humanity cannot contain the pure, raw, concentrated essence of the living God. What a great joy when we will behold Him "face to face."

Things happen when you start asking God to reveal His glory. Things happen when you start seeking after the presence of God. Things happen when God responds to our heart cries—we are never the same again. We may not be able to withstand the fullness of all of His glory, but this passage shows us that God will still reveal to us a measure of His glory that will leave us changed forever.

The apostle Paul was unable to describe an encounter he had when God's glory and presence showed up. He said he was "caught up" into the third heaven and heard "inexpressible words" (2 Cor. 12:1–6). Paul was just a man, but he had a hunger, a deep insatiable hunger that said, "I want more of You, Lord!"

God's children with pure hearts do experience visions of God that are enigmas to the worldly mind, and incomprehensible to the carnal heart.

But for the holy person these bring heaven to earth while the longing still remains for the glories of heaven.

— LEO G. COX[1]

God's glory still shows up in places where He is welcomed and sought after. He still answers the call of hungry hearts. Glimpses of His glory still leave us scrambling for words to describe what happened. Many times it is indescribable—because our senses are taking it in through every dimension. The old adage "You had to be there" is often true of these types of visitations. We just need to be there, pouring our hearts out before Him saying, "God, show me Your way and show me Your glory!"

I am so hungry for more than what I have seen and experienced. I praise the Lord for all of it, but something tells me there is more. Every wonderful encounter with God strengthens me for the next challenge. As long as His presence goes with me, I know I am ready.

Part 2

A Praise That's All My Own

Words & Music: David M. Edwards & Margaret Becker*

Verse 1:
I will not offer a blemished sacrifice
Nor give you praise for which I have not paid the price
Greater than the angels who make the sweetest sound
I bring a heart to worship and a life that's poured out

Chorus:
A praise that's all my own
Something fitting for a king
What a debt I owe
To your endless love for me
How I long to bring
A praise that costs me everything
A praise that's all my own

Verse 2:
Oil of adoration poured upon your feet
I'm not ashamed to worship with tears that I weep
Nothing will deter me—I know what I must do
I'll lay my life on your altar and worship only you

Chapter 4

Putting On Praise

§ § §

One of my favorite verses in the Bible is Proverbs 16:32: "He who is slow to anger is better than the mighty, and he who rules his spirit than he who takes a city" (NKJV). Solomon realized that self-discipline is more important—and more difficult—than physical strength and ability. Later, Paul wrote, "For God has not given us a spirit of fear, but of power and of love and of a sound mind" (2 Tim. 1:7 NKJV). Sound mind means self-control and self-discipline.

With God's strength and help, through the indwelling presence of His Holy Spirit who lives inside every born-again person, we can set the tone for our day. In fact, self-control is a by-product of our relationship with the Holy Spirit. It is referred to in Galatians as part of the fruit of the Holy Spirit that is produced in the life of the believer.

Because the Holy Spirit enables us to "rule our spirits" or to have self-control, you and I have a profound impact on setting the tone for our day. We have the spiritual capability to bless or curse each day. We have to make a choice each day how we will proceed through that day. You and I must make a choice at the outset of every situation: will this ruin my day? or is this an opportunity for God to move? To a large degree, we can control to what extent it will affect us.

Most of our negative thoughts come from our constantly repeating the lies of the enemy. Rather than training our spirits to rule well and be self-controlled, we have trained our human spirits to repeat the negative garbage of this world. The bulk of oppressive and depressive thoughts are the fiery darts of the enemy that arrive to greet us when we wake up every morning.

Some people get up every morning and begin thinking negative thoughts from the moment their feet hit the ground. "Oh, I hate going to work. . . . I wish I didn't have to get up. . . . I don't want to go to church, I've been working all week. . . . Why do I bother?" Sound familiar? We can get into a habit of doing it without even realizing that we are setting the tone for our day. We are thinking negatively about our day before it begins.

In essence, we are saying to the devil, "Yes, I agree with you that this is going to be a bad day and I'm going to hate it. Thank you, Satan, for reminding me that I'm trash and I'm nothing to everyone." Now I know this seems silly, but you know it's true. We do this kind of stuff every day. God's Word would never tell us to continually confess and dwell on negative things about our situation or ourselves. So then, where do those kinds of thoughts come from? Who is behind such words? It certainly isn't God.

A Spirit of Heaviness

All these negative thoughts can develop to such a degree that they become a form of depression. Have you ever felt like you didn't want to get out of bed in the morning? I know I have. There are times when the lies of the enemy try to convince us that life is not worth living, nobody needs us, nobody cares. It can build up over time or it can come out of nowhere. All of these things point to a spirit of heaviness.

Have you ever met someone with a spirit of heaviness? You ask, "How are you doing today?" He responds, "Don't ask." You say, "Hey, how's it going?" She replies, "It's going." We sometimes say that a person has "the blues," but what that person really has is a spirit—a spirit of heaviness. When you get depressed, when you start to feel sorry for yourself, when you are going through a darkness, a time of obscurity and feebleness, that's the spirit of heaviness. There is an enemy of your soul who will do anything to discourage and destroy you. It's a spirit sent from hell! But, praise God, there's a cure. . . .

The Spirit of the Lord GOD is upon Me,
Because the LORD has anointed Me
To preach good tidings to the poor;
He has sent Me to heal the brokenhearted,
To proclaim liberty to the captives,
And the opening of the prison to those who are bound;
To proclaim the acceptable year of the LORD,
And the day of vengeance of our God;
To comfort all who mourn,
To console those who mourn in Zion,
To give them beauty for ashes,
The oil of joy for mourning,
The garment of praise for the spirit of heaviness;
That they may be called trees of righteousness,
The planting of the LORD, that He may be glorified."
(Isa. 61:1–3 NKJV, emphasis added)

"The garment of praise for the spirit of heaviness"—the Hebrew word for *heaviness* means "distressed, full of heaviness, brokenhearted, affliction of self, depression, feeble, obscure, darkish." Do you recognize a time that you have been afflicted with a spirit of heaviness? If you have one now, read on. If you should ever encounter the spirit of heaviness, I'm going to tell you how to deal with it.

You Must Choose to Put On Praise

The only way to replace the spirit of heaviness is to put on the garment of praise. We must choose to put on praise. Just as we choose to say the negative things that the enemy is feeding us, we can choose to put on praise instead. Praise is a garment that we are to wear. Jesus, through the power of His Holy Spirit, provides it, but it is our responsibility to put it on. It's there for us but will do us no good unless we use it. Let's dig a little deeper. . . . "My soul melts from heaviness; strengthen me according to Your word" (Ps. 119:28 NKJV). How are we strengthened? We are made strong by the Word of God. What God's Word says about our lives and our situation will strengthen us. *When heaviness shows up, start praising God for His promises.*

> *The only way to replace the spirit of heaviness is to put on the garment of praise!*

"Anxiety in the heart of a man causes depression, but a good word makes it glad" (Prov. 12:25 NKJV). We've all been there, when everything seems to be crashing in around us, when the odds are stacked against us, when we are at the proverbial end of the rope. I have had to learn the hard way that even when I don't feel like it, I need to praise Him anyway. There is power in praising God—He has promised to inhabit our praise. Even when I am not sensing His presence, I need to praise Him because He has a proven track record of *always* coming through. This is when godly character must kick in and do the right thing whether we feel like it or not. And the right thing is to put on the garment of praise. You've probably seen the TV commercial that promotes the cereal Wheaties as the "breakfast of champions." Even more than our needing Wheaties in the morning, we need to put on praise. What would our day look like if we met the morning with praise and began to thank God from the outset for who He is, what He's done, and what He has promised to do? The spirit of heaviness wants you to get up and begin the day with a new string of negative thoughts. But you can turn that around by jumping out of bed and proclaiming, "This is the day the Lord has made; I will rejoice and be glad in it!" The more you continue to praise God, the fainter the lies of the enemy become because you are feeding your faith and starving your doubts by putting on the garment of praise.

> *You need to be putting on praise. God's not going to put it on you.*

You need to be putting on praise. God's not going to put it on you. I can't put it on you. Your church can't put it on you—even if everyone around you is clapping, praising, shouting, and dancing. You must decide to put it on for yourself. You can't be using someone else's testimony or someone else's praise—*your* praise must come from inside of *you*. Each of us needs to put on the garment of praise.

The Power of Speech

Jesus reminds us in Matthew 12:34 that "the mouth speaks from the overflow of the heart." What's in your heart today? I can tell when I haven't been in the Word like I should. I can also tell when I haven't been spending time in God's presence like I should. How can I tell? I can detect it in my speech. When I start getting negative or critical, I can almost always trace it to one of those two things. When I have been in God's Word like I should and when I'm spending personal time with God in His presence like I should, I don't speak like that.

We reflect what we behold. And if I am beholding the Lord and His Word, my life and speech will reflect that.

I want to mirror Him and all that He is. It doesn't matter if you've been a Christian for thirty days or thirty years, the enemy's tactics are pretty consistent (because they work): he attacks us in our minds. The devil brings fear, tries to sow doubt, and unleashes discouragement. In other words, all the things God would *never* tell you the devil will—and he does.

> *We reflect what we behold!*

For instance, one of the first things many Christians experience after being saved is the cynical little voice that comes and says, "You're not saved!" Sound familiar? Of course it does because he does it to everyone. It is the same broken record—a number-one hit in hell: "You're not saved." "You're not called to ministry." "God's not going to use *you*." "Look what you used to do." "You're not filled with the Holy Spirit." The lies go on and on, and as creatures of habit, if we repeat the lies long enough, we start to believe them.

That is why it is so important to repeat what God's Word says. When we praise and worship God, we should use Scripture all the time. Whether we are reading it, speaking it, singing it, or shouting it, God's Word is powerful. By saying God's Word aloud, you will find that it has an undeniable effect upon you and your situation.

"Life and death are in the power of the tongue, and those who love it will eat its fruit" (Prov. 18:21). When we speak God's Word, we are speaking "life," and when we speak the lies of the enemy, we are speaking "death." Remember that God *spoke* the worlds into existence. Words are powerful things. Our words can bless or curse. Our words can heal or hurt. Our words can bring inclusion or isolation. We need to let the power of God's Word heal us and others.

My son, pay attention to my words;
listen closely to my sayings.
Don't lose sight of them;

keep them within your heart.
For they are life to those who find them,
and health to one's whole body.
Guard your heart above all else,
for it is the source of life. (Prov. 4:20–23)

God's Word can even have an impact upon our physiology. Doctors treat patients every day who have been wounded and destroyed by the words of others. Of course, it is Satan behind all of it doing what he does best—kill, steal, and destroy. You and I have felt the pain of words spoken against us and we have witnessed first-hand the damage they can do. But how much more power would our speech have if it were God's holy Word spoken under the unction of the Holy Spirit! That would stop the enemy dead in his tracks. And it will bring healing to our spirits, souls, and bodies.

"For the word of God is living and effective and sharper than any two-edged sword, penetrating as far as to divide soul, spirit, joints, and marrow; it is a judge of the ideas and thoughts of the heart" (Heb. 4:12). When we spend time in God's Word in our personal worship time with Him, the Holy Spirit will use it like a scalpel to separate and surgically remove those things that hinder our growth in Christ Jesus. And because of Jesus' shed blood, we can confess those things, be forgiven of them, and draw closer still. That is worship! That is relationship!

Furthermore, His spoken Word in our mouth becomes a sword against the enemy and his lies. "Take the helmet of salvation, and the sword of the Spirit, which is God's word" (Eph. 6:17). *God's word* is not the Greek word *logos*, which means "written word"; it is the Greek word *rhema*, which means "spoken word." In Paul's teaching about the believer's armor, the only offensive weapon he mentions is the Word of God. God's Word in our mouth, spoken out loud in our

> *We also have a spiritual decision to make every morning about what we will wear: will I or won't I put on my garment of praise?*

prayer and praise becomes a sufficient weapon against the evil one and all of his negative attacks. This is a powerful truth. No other weapon against the enemy is in this list in Ephesians except the Word of God in our mouths. The trouble is, we don't use it like we should or as often as we should. If we did, how potent the ranks of the redeemed would be!

So instead of repeating the enemy's lies, let's start repeating the "good word" that is God's Word and make our hearts glad. Lord, let us be strengthened according to Your word.

What's in Your Praise Wardrobe?

One of the first things we decide in the morning is what we're going to wear. We get up and put some clothes on. Sometimes we put some thought into it, other times we just throw on sweatpants and a T-shirt. We also have a spiritual decision to make every morning about what we will wear: will I or won't I put on my garment of praise? I have even found that we can fine-tune our wardrobe for any occasion. God has given us plenty of options.

Each morning, we need to get up, open our praise wardrobe, and say, "What should I wear today?" Our attitude needs to be *I'm not going to be depressed today; I'm not going to be negative today; I'm not going to be Satan's punching bag today. I'm going to put on my garment of praise.* You might pull out this outfit:

"No weapon formed against you will succeed,
and you will refute any accusation
raised against you in court.
This is the heritage of the Lord's servants,
and their righteousness is from Me." (Isa. 54:17)

Or you might try on one of these:
    "Do not fear, for I have redeemed you;
    I have called you by your name;
        you are Mine.
    I will be with you
    when you pass through the waters,
    and when you pass through the rivers,
    they will not overwhelm you.
    You will not be scorched
    when you walk through the fire,
    and the flame will not burn you." (Isa. 43:1–2)

    But those who trust in the LORD
    will renew their strength;
    they will soar on wings like eagles;
    they will run and not grow weary;
    they will walk and not faint. (Isa. 40:31)

This praise garment has helped me before:
    Oh, give thanks to the LORD, for He is good!
    For His mercy endures forever. (Ps. 136:1 NKJV)

What about starting your day with these?
    I will give You thanks with all my heart;
    I will sing Your praise before the heavenly beings.
    (Ps. 138:1)

    My soul, praise the LORD,
    and all that is within me, praise His holy name.
    My soul, praise the LORD,
    and do not forget all His benefits. (Ps. 103:1–2)

I wore this garment of praise when I didn't know how I'd pay the bills:
    And my God will supply all your needs according to His riches in glory in Christ Jesus. (Phil. 4:19)

I wore this when I didn't think I could make it:
> I am able to do all things through Him who strengthens me. (Phil. 4:13)

I wore this when the disconcerting doctor's report came in:
> He Himself bore our sins
> in His body on the tree,
> so that, having died to sins,
> we might live for righteousness;
> by His wounding you have been healed. (1 Pet. 2:24)

There's so much to wear, so many garments of praise. Our "praise wardrobe" is full of eternal garments that will never go out of style. Our biggest problem will be picking which one to put on. If you want to dress for success, you must know how to bless! Here are a few more:
> I will praise the LORD at all times;
> His praise will always be on my lips. (Ps. 34:1)

> Taste and see that the LORD is good.
> How happy is the man who takes refuge in Him!"
> (Ps. 34:8)

> God, be exalted above the heavens;
> let Your glory be above the whole earth. (Ps. 57:5)

Don't tell me you don't have anything to wear. You've been looking in the wrong wardrobe. You have more outfits than you'll wear in a lifetime. Have you ever met someone who changes clothes three or four times a day? Well, with your personal "praise wardrobe," you can wear as many outfits a day as you want—and there's no laundry to do. They are self-cleansing.

You may think my metaphor of a "praise wardrobe" is silly, but it's grounded in truth. Sometimes we miss the simple things of God because we become too analytical about Scripture. It's not brain surgery. Speaking God's Word works—period. It will not only change you, but it will change your family, your ministry, your job, your friends—and the list goes on.

> *There is something blessed about the person who has learned to love and treasure the Word of God.*

There is something blessed about the person who has learned to love and treasure the Word of God. People will want to be around you because the world hungers to hear something good, something hopeful, merciful, loving; something life changing. People will experience the healing effect of God's Word as you and I live it and speak it. Furthermore, just think of the annihilating results it will have on the attacks of the enemy as well. We must remember that it is a "two-edged sword."

Now, aren't you sorry for all those times you walked around with a spirit of heaviness when you could've been sporting a garment of praise? You and God could have been putting on a praise fashion show—and God wants to put on a praise fashion show in your life. As you praise Him, that praise opens the door for Him to work. It opens the door for God to show off miracle after miracle in you. It gives Him the opportunity to run your day. He will walk you down the "fashion runway" of life, putting to shame every enemy in sight.

When we praise God, it scatters the enemy. Your praise lets hell know every day who they're dealing with. Remember, the One in you is greater than the one who is in the world (1 John 4:4). The devil is a liar and God is on the throne.

It's Your Choice

Remember, life and death are in the power of the tongue. You and I can speak either death or life over ourselves. It's our choice. We can choose to declare life's negatives, declare defeat, complain constantly, talk about how big the devil is, and so on, or we can speak life, which is praising God, speaking His Word, declaring that even when a rough spot comes along, God will deliver us.

Wrap yourself in praise. Clothe your home in God's praises. Open the Bible, the praise wardrobe, and begin to put on something supernatural. Then just watch the spirit of heaviness try to get through that.

"A man's spirit can endure sickness, but who can survive a broken spirit?" (Prov. 18:14). A "broken spirit" is when someone's personhood or personality has been crushed beneath the weight of heartache, disappointment, and life's hardships. A "broken spirit" can also result in depression or being oppressed. Let me give you some good news today: Jesus Christ specializes in healing people from the inside out. Jesus is the answer to what ails us.

The praise of God and the repeating of His promises have a profound healing effect upon our human spirits. I realized long ago that if we are to make it through difficult times, we'd better have a powerful weapon in our arsenal. The devil knows all about it, and so should we.

Let's put on the garment of praise right now. Hell's negative energy cannot operate in an atmosphere of praise. Hell's "anti-hope" agenda doesn't work on people who wear the garment of praise. Get rid of the spirit of heaviness right now in your life. Start praising God right where you are. Put on the garment of praise!

Chapter 5

The Power of Praise

§ § §

*T*hings happen when we worship the Lord. Worship becomes a tool of warfare in the believer's arsenal to combat the forces of darkness. The praises of the living God dismantle and disengage the threats and traps of the enemy of our souls. In order for us to advance the kingdom of our God, we must *sustain* a spirit of worship to Him. Our worship creates an invisible base whereby He begins to work because He lives within (inhabits) the praises of His people (the redeemed). When God is at home (in praise), He is free to move about. As my heart (spirit) and will (soul) cooperate with His desires, He can rule and reign through my worship.

Consequently, worship cannot merely be lip service, but needs to grow into a lifestyle of praise to God. There is no power in lip service. Lip service is simply words directed to someone with whom the one doing the talking has no relationship. There is never any power in faking a relationship with God. As I worship Him from a heart that is surrendered to Him, my enemies will not prevail over me because my praise infuses the situation with Kingdom power.

We must never forget that God grows the church through spiritual power—not programs, not media events, not machinery, not seminars, not conventions. His Word declares, "For the kingdom of God is not in talk but in power" (1 Cor. 4:20). In other words, talk is cheap, but speech that emanates from a relationship with God has power and authority because it is rooted in what we know to be true. Our ability to stand against evil is found in kneeling first at His feet in worship and surrender. He is our power supply, our strength, our all in all. He is the Captain of the Hosts.

A wonderful friend of mine, Sally Morgenthaler, wrote an article several years ago that illustrates further what I'm talking about.

When David was a boy he learned what a slingshot could do, and he operated it bravely and effectively long before he confronted Goliath. Yet, we dare not forget that David went into battle with much more than target practice under his belt. He went with spiritual power, a power rooted in his worship relationship with God. For, it was in that relationship of unfettered devotion that God molded David's heart, sculpting a humble and ready dependence on divine knowledge and strength, and an unquenchable desire to give God every bit of the glory. And just as God was more interested in David's heart than in his capabilities, so it is with us. God does not ask, "How much can you do for me and how well, accurately and bravely can you do it?" Rather, God asks, "Whose are you, for whom will you do all these good things, and on whom will you depend?" In a word, God asks for our worship! And in the final analysis, we are either Davids, worshipers with a ready slingshot, or slingshot experts with just enough worship to make us acceptably pious. There is no doubt which one God prefers.[1]

God not only wants to mold our hearts as individuals, but God wants His people—the church—to have the heart of worshipers. God has always longed for His people to be worshipers, and He has revealed down through the ages the benefits that come from having such a heart. One of those benefits, besides being a spiritual truth, is: God's presence is manifested in praise and worship. And His presence will always equal victory. "But You are holy, enthroned on the praises of Israel" (Ps. 22:3). Whenever and wherever God's people praise Him, their praise establishes a place for Him to rule and reign from. And it follows that when God is ruling and reigning, many wonderful things are going to take place. After a victorious battle, Moses gave God the glory and the credit for the children of Israel's victory. In Exodus 17:15, God revealed through Moses a unique name for Himself, "The Lord Is My Banner" (*Jehovah Nissi*). "The Lord Is My Banner" also means "The Lord Our Victory," or "The Lord Our Miracle." This forever secures victory for God's people because His very name means victory! Our victory in spiritual battles will come as we rely upon the Lord to fight on our behalf. This is what it means to trust the Lord in battle and stand still to see His deliverance.

> *God has always longed for His people to be worshipers, and He has revealed down through the ages the benefits that come from having such a heart.*

The size of our enemy is irrelevant; it's the size of our ally—it's the size of our God that matters.

Go Down before Getting Up

To me, no other victory in the history of Israel more vividly portrays and reveals the importance of praise and worship in the midst of the battle than the account of King Jehoshaphat found in 2 Chronicles 20. King Jehoshaphat was the great-

great grandson of Solomon and reigned for twenty-five years. When faced with the greatest crisis of his life, King Jehoshaphat learned an important lesson about the power of praise.

Three different nations, the Moabites, Ammonites, and others from Edom, were coming against Jehoshaphat and the people of Judah—and they were coming to wipe them out. The King had reports from his lookouts that the army coming against him was a vast and great multitude.

> *The size of our enemy is irrelevant; it's the size of our ally— it's the size of our God!*

Now, what would you do if that kind of report came your way? I don't know, of course, but I do know this: the way you respond will make a big difference in how the situation ultimately develops—yes, even before it *starts* to develop. And even if things go differently than you want or expect, you will be putting yourself in a position to see it more clearly from God's perspective. Look at 2 Chronicles 20:3—"Jehoshaphat was afraid, so he resolved to seek the LORD. So he proclaimed a fast for all Judah."

Before you ever do anything about a situation—before you make a move based on your emotions, before you respond to negative news, before you take on the enemy— you must get down on your knees and give it to God. We must go down before we get up. This should always be our response to bad news.

I am so thankful for my parents, who taught me to go down before getting up. In the course of all of our lives, we are faced with tragedy, challenge, and testing—it is a part of life. But when bad news came to our house, my mom and dad always took it to the Lord. We would praise God for the answer before we ever "saw" the answer. When I went on to college and called home with my own concerns about the challenges I was facing, again they would remind me to take it to the Lord first and praise Him for the victory—even before victory came.

We must train ourselves to go to God first. Our tendency is to immediately try to fix things ourselves, but we must counter that by getting down on our knees before the Lord and laying it out before Him. We are always trying to help God out but never know what the battle plan is because we have been too busy trying to fix what lies beyond our

> We must go down before we get up.

reach, repair what only prayer can, and fight battles without a song. God does have a plan and He will let you in on it—just ask Him. Before you *do* anything, go to God first.

Jehoshaphat, like David and Solomon before him, took it to the Lord. He came from a line of worshipers, and here again another king gets off his throne and bows low before the King of all kings and pours out his heart to the only One who can make a difference. Jehoshaphat began to seek the Lord through fasting, he gathered together others to pray and fast, he confessed his helplessness, he obeyed the Holy Spirit, he put his trust in the Lord and in His Word, and then he gave thanks to the Lord *before the battle ever took place!* He did all of these things *before* things got out of hand— before he could feel the heat coming from the breath of his enemies, he went down on his knees in worship.

The Presence of God Equals Victory

When faced with this serious situation, Jehoshaphat went to the Lord in prayer. His prayer and God's subsequent response are full of powerful truths that give us insight into the relationship between worship and warfare.

Then Jehoshaphat stood in the assembly of Judah and Jerusalem in the LORD's temple before the new courtyard. He said:

LORD God of our ancestors, are You not the God who is in heaven, and do You not rule over all the kingdoms of the nations? Power and might are in Your hand, and no one can stand against You. Are You not our God who drove out the inhabitants of this land before Your people Israel and who gave it forever to the descendents of Abraham Your friend? They have lived in the land and have built You a sanctuary in it for Your name and have said, "If disaster comes on us— sword or judgment, pestilence or famine—we will stand before this temple and before You, for Your name is in this temple. We will cry out to You because of our distress, and You will hear and deliver." . . .

Our God, will You not judge them? For we are powerless before this vast multitude that comes [to fight] against us. We do not know what to do, but we look to You. (2 Chron. 20:5–9, 12)

I want to examine quickly three things that King Jehoshaphat established in his prayer to the Lord. First, he praised, confessed, and declared that God is omnipotent over all and no one can stand against His power or in the way of His will. Second, he praised God for His faithfulness—His track record—to His people in the past and in the present. And finally, he confessed that there was nothing they could do in and of themselves to change the situation—they were totally surrendered to God for His help, mercy, and deliverance.

The next thing that happened was that God spoke back. Did you know that if you go to God in prayer with a sincere heart, He will respond? God answers. God has a word for you. God has a word for your situation. Even today, many times the voice of the Holy Spirit shows up after God's people come before Him to worship and confess their utter dependency upon Him. God speaks back!

The Holy Spirit came upon Jahaziel and he began to give the word of the Lord for Jehoshaphat's situation. Let's look at what God said:

All Judah was standing before the LORD with their infants, their wives, and their children. In the midst of the congregation, the Spirit of the LORD came on Jahaziel (son of Zechariah, son of Benaiah, son of Jeiel, son of Mattaniah, a Levite from Asaph's descendants), and he said, "Listen carefully, all Judah and you inhabitants of Jerusalem, and King Jehoshaphat. This is what the LORD says: 'Do not be afraid or discouraged because of this vast multitude, for *the battle is not yours, but God's.* Tomorrow, go down against them. You will see them coming up the ascent of Ziz, and you will find them at the end of the valley facing the Wilderness of Jeruel. *You do not have to fight this [battle]. Position yourselves, stand still, and see the salvation of the LORD.* [He is] with you, Judah and Jerusalem. Do not be afraid or discouraged. Tomorrow, *go out to face them, for the LORD is with you.'"*

Then Jehoshaphat bowed with his face to the ground, and all Judah and the inhabitants of Jerusalem fell down before the LORD to worship Him. Then the Levites from the sons of the Kohathites and the Korahites *stood up to praise the LORD God of Israel shouting in a loud voice.* (2 Chron. 20:13–19, emphasis added)

The bottom line here: God's presence among His people will always equal victory. Greater is He that is in us than he that is in this world. God *never* loses; He never quits or sleeps. God *always* wins; He always prevails and leads us in triumph!

Praise—An Instrument of Warfare

I want to pay close attention to the fact that after God had spoken and given them direction, *they worshiped Him again.* The battle still hadn't happened—but they went ahead and worshiped Him because they realized a great spiritual truth: you must fight the battle in the spiritual realm first and win there before you can win it in the natural realm. "For though we walk in the flesh, we do not war according to the flesh. For the weapons of our warfare are not carnal but mighty in God for pulling down strongholds" (2 Cor. 10:3–4 NKJV). We must learn to employ and believe in praise as a mighty, effectual spiritual weapon.

> *We must learn to employ and believe in praise as a mighty, effectual spiritual weapon.*

After they worshiped again, the next morning King Jehoshaphat reminded his people of God's Word. Why? Because God does not lie—He keeps His Word. This was going to be one "Holy War" that would top them all. These people had no idea about the size of the victory that God was going to hand them. And many times, we usually have no idea about the vastness and greatness of victory that God longs to give us. If we will go down before we go up, and if we will worship and praise Him first, we will see victory on a level we have never experienced before.

Now before we get on with the story, we need to understand that when God said, "stand still," that didn't mean "do nothing." Though they weren't fighting per se, they did *continue* to praise and worship the Lord, and He made their praise His permanent address that day as He wiped out their enemies before them. So many times we miss winning our battles because we just say, "Oh, the battle belongs to the Lord. You just have to be still," and we have mistaken "still" for doing nothing. If you are doing nothing, you will never see victory. You must create a habitation for the Lord in your praise.

God taught His people that day that their praise to Him is also an instrument of warfare against the enemy of their souls. *Praise is an instrument of warfare.* The "praisers" went out before the army—just like they praised Him for victory before the battle took place. No one was going to get the credit for this victory except God and God alone.

In the morning they got up early and went out to the wilderness of Tekoa. As they were about to go out, Jehoshaphat stood and said, "Hear me, Judah and you inhabitants of Jerusalem. Believe in the LORD your God, and you will be established; believe in His prophets, and you will succeed." Then he consulted with the people and appointed *some to sing for the LORD* and *some to praise the splendor of [His] holiness*. When *they went out in front of the armed forces*, they *kept singing*:

Give thanks to the LORD,
for His faithful love endures forever.

The moment they began [their] shouts and praises, the LORD set an ambush against the Ammonites, Moabites and [the inhabitants of] Mount Seir who came [to fight] against Judah, and they were defeated. The Ammonites and Moabites turned against the inhabitants of Mount Seir and completely annihilated them. When they had finished with the inhabitants of Seir, they helped destroy each other.

When Judah came to a place overlooking the wilderness, they looked toward the multitude, and there were corpses lying on the ground; *nobody had escaped.* (2 Chron. 20:20–24, emphasis added).

"The battle is not yours, but God's" was the encouraging word presented to King Jehoshaphat before the battle had begun. The reward of faith is always security and success. All they had to do—all we have to do—was obey God and put their faith in His Word. You can't help but notice as well that Jehoshaphat appointed one praise team just to sing to the Lord and another praise team to just concentrate their praises on the splendor of His holiness. Wow! Everybody heard God's praises that day.

A Symbol or the Real Thing?

This was literally a "holy war." Instead of the usual battle strategy that would send the ark of the covenant into war ahead of the people, this time God sent the worship team in first. Up to that time, the ark was the symbol of God's presence, but now God's presence was coming out of the box and going to take up residence in the very atmosphere of their praise.

Can you imagine being on the praise team and showing up that morning? The worship leader stands up and says something like: "Well, we're going to try something new today. I'm sure you all have heard of the sizable armies just over the ridge that we'll be taking on today. They have the latest in tank equipment, air power, and armaments. However, the General thought it would be a great idea for you—the praise team—to go in first instead of the army's tanks. In fact, you will have no weapons to carry and no protection whatsoever. It'll be really cool. What do you think?" How would you like to have been on that worship team?

God did not want them relying on a symbol of worship; He wanted them to rely on Him! Their faith needed to be in Him, not what was in the ark. Too many times we rely on our past experiences to get us through the now, and it's simply not going to work. We need a fresh "word from God" every day. We need a fresh revelation of what God is doing in our lives. We need to quit worshiping the past and what God used to do and used to say and the way He used to move, and get with the praise program and begin to realize that the battle was never ours, but God's. Don't get caught up in the symbols of His presence when you could be caught up in Him. I want the real thing; how about you?

Instead of the ark, the Levites headed the army, singing, "Praise the Lord, for His faithful love endures forever." Just as God promised, His people did not need to lift a finger—they just lifted up praise. Internal strife erupted among the attacking enemy ranks and they turned on one another, killing each other. Not one of their enemies escaped alive. God gave Jehoshaphat his greatest victory. True to His nature, God kept His word.

> *Praise is an instrument of warfare!*

Maybe right now God is saying the same thing to you: "Do not be afraid nor dismayed because of the great multitude of your enemies; this battle is not yours, but Mine. Lift your hands and praise Me!"

The enemy was so confounded by the praises of God that they turned on one another until there was *not one enemy left*! Think of it—when God's people praised Him, not one of their enemies was able to escape. When those people began to sing and praise God, they had an expectancy that God would fight for them. That expectancy is called *faith*.

The soldiers of Jehoshaphat's army plundered the dead bodies of their enemies for three days, collecting more jewels and valuables than they could carry away. The return to Jerusalem was a joyous occasion for all Judah. The children of God returned to Jerusalem, singing and playing their instruments to the Lord—and good King Jehoshaphat led the way. They assembled at the house of the Lord, where they offered up more praise and thanksgiving to God for giving them the victory over their enemies. He had indeed fought the battle for them. As word spread of what God had done for Judah, other countries decided to leave them alone. I wonder why?

Singing into Battle

What can you and I learn from Judah's "praise-produced victory"? The most obvious lesson is that the strength and power of faith are demonstrated by praising God in song in the face of battle. We need to keep this in mind whether we are praising God alone in our daily worship or gathered together as a choir of soldiers in church. We can have huge victories over our enemies when we worship and praise the Lord. Every time we gather as a congregation, our worship should be a death warrant to hell's working force in our homes and communities. We need to get with the program—the Praise Program.

> *Your praise will crowd out everything else that's vying for your attention. Your praise will crowd out every other thought but Jesus!*

If you go singing into battle . . . you'll hear your praise song above the enemy's voice. If you go singing into battle . . . you'll hear your praise song above the enemy's artillery. If you go singing into battle . . . your praise song to the Lord will have a soothing effect on your mind, will, and emotions (soul). Your praise will crowd out everything else that's vying for your attention. Your praise will crowd out every other thought but thoughts of Jesus. Of course, you cannot sing praises and talk defeat at the same time. If you're singing to God, there's no room for negative statements like "If I ignore this, maybe it will go away," or "The devil has me beaten." When you're singing to God, you're not speaking doubt and fear, as in "God, I hope You know what You're doing," or "There's no hope."

Go ahead and sing to God with a voice of triumph. Drown out hell's lies and murmurings. Put your faith in the One who loves you and calls you by name.

The Devil Hates Praise

God has appointed (ordained) praise because it stops the enemy dead in his tracks. Neither the devil nor his demons can offer any kind of protest after praise. They are silenced. The devil and his demons hate praise and they live in misery. Their only temporary relief is found in inflicting like misery on human beings, who were created in the image of God. Praise produces panic and fear within hell's demonic ranks.

Satan hates praise. Yet, he desired the praise and adoration that God received for Himself and was kicked out of heaven. He even asked Jesus to bow down and worship him (Matt. 4:9). Can you imagine? Even knowing that his future in the abyss was secure, his evil pride and arrogance couldn't resist belittling the Son of God.

Jack Taylor, in his wonderful book *The Hallelujah Factor* writes:

> Praise is . . . forever etched into the memory banks of Satan and his demons, i.e., fallen angels. They, as so few in the universe, knew the powers, joys, and delights of praise. When they hear Biblical praises they are stricken with fear and panic. They are irritated and devastated. They probably turn on each other in hatred and frustration, like Jehoshaphat's enemies did. Like fingernails on a chalkboard is the sound of praises to hell. Their anger, hatred, and panic reach a boiling point. Just like jailed accomplices hate each other, so the demons despise each other because of their stupidity in cooperating with the devil in bringing them to their demise. They scream against the Praised and the praisers, seeking anyway to silence the adoration of God that they hate so much. Their ranks broken, they are devastated by praise. Their influence is neutralized and their lies are exposed by praise.[2]

At the first sign of trouble, we must not run and hide. We need to go down on our knees in worship and praise the

Lord with everything we have, then get up and stand in the strength He provides as we continue to praise. He established this weapon of warfare for us a long time ago: "O LORD, our Lord, how majestic is your name in all the earth! You have set your glory above the heavens. From the lips of children and infants you have ordained praise because of your enemies, to silence the foe and the avenger" (Ps. 8:1–2 NIV).

God wants to give us a new mentality regarding the devil and his works. Instead of seeing the devil as a threat to us, we need to see ourselves as his worst nightmare. We are the threat to his kingdom and the object of his fear. We are no longer going to be in a defensive position awaiting his attack; rather, we are going to take the offensive and go after him and his evil kingdom with a passion.

The Praise Program

We need to get with what I call the Praise Program. The praisers in Jehoshaphat's army proclaimed only one powerful sentence of praise: "Give thanks to the LORD, for His faithful love endures forever!" The words *faithful love* mean *mercy*. Mercy is God's unfailing kindness and tenderness and is His active desire to remove distress from us. Just imagine being under attack anywhere and shouting out a praise to God. Demons would go hurling into the darkness. Get your double-barreled praise gun out. You need to be packing some *real* heat.

Praise scatters the enemy. We need to get with God's Praise Program. Go ahead and say it out loud, "I subscribe to the Praise Program! When the devil starts messing with me, I'll shout to God with a voice of triumph!"

When we praise the Lord for His love for us and His desire to deliver us, our praise ignites our heavenly Father's will to crush our enemies, and that will becomes action on our behalf. What is it in your life that needs deliverance today? Where are you being pressed in upon by the forces of hell? If you'll acknowledge Him and praise Him right now, wherever you are, God will give you the victory. Your mouth is a powerful weapon—use it wisely.

Get with the Praise Program and watch God wipe out every enemy in sight. Besides, the battle isn't yours—it's His. The results of praise will always leave the enemy strewn across the battlefield and the battlefield will always yield its fruit and bounty. It took Jehoshaphat's army three days to collect all of the treasure, then they again came before the Lord to lift up their praise and worship Him.

They praised Him before the battle, they praised Him during the battle, and they praised Him after the battle. And the greatest result of praise is found in 2 Chronicles 20:30, "Then Jehoshaphat's kingdom was quiet, for his God gave him rest on every side." You see, the end result of their praise and confidence in God—the end result of God fighting for them—was rest. And rest equals peace, peace that can only be found in His presence.

The presence of God always equals victory. Before we ever come to victory, we must get into position for it—we must go down before we can go up. There is great power in praise. How do we get into position for victory?

- Covet the presence of God.
- Depend upon His presence when confronting any opposition.
- Know that the battle is not yours, but His.
- Trust the Lord to do your fighting for you.
- Sustain His rule and reign through praise.

Chapter 6

The Sacrifice of Praise

§ § §

The Old Covenant and its sacrificial system were but types and shadows of what was to come under the New Covenant, established by the sacrificial death and resurrection of Jesus Christ. In order to fully appreciate what is ours by faith through grace, it is important to understand what preceded it all. When we understand the "how" and "what" of worship under the Old Covenant, it deepens our appreciation for and understanding of our worship on this side of the cross. The book of Hebrews goes to great lengths to explain all of this "type and shadow" imagery.

Jesus Christ has become both our High Priest and our sin sacrifice. He replaced an imperfect priesthood and accomplished once and for all what the Old Covenant sacrificial system was powerless to do, through the offering of His own body and blood. Still, there are spiritual and eternal meanings to many things that took place in Israel's tabernacle and temple worship.

One of those special "types and shadows" that took place under the Old Covenant and continues today under the New Covenant is what is called a "sacrifice of praise" or a "thank offering." Thank offerings would be offered out of sheer gratitude and thankfulness to the Lord (Lev. 7:11–15). It was both spontaneous and intentional, and God no doubt enjoyed them so very much because they were not required. They must have been offered up for a million different reasons by millions of different people who wanted to thank the Lord for something, honor Him for a specific reason, and share their love of Him just because.

"Whoever sacrifices a thank offering honors Me,
and whoever orders his conduct,
I will show him the salvation of God." (Ps. 50:23)

There is something God-honoring about a thank offering. It is a sacrifice that it is not required, yet it releases the power and blessing of God to move in a special way in the life of the one doing the sacrificing. And I am sure that the one doing the sacrificing finds a greater joy and a deeper walk with the Lord as a result of such an offering. God loves the sacrifice of praise.

Thus says the LORD: "Again *there shall be heard in this place* . . . the voice of joy and the voice of gladness, the voice of the bridegroom and the voice of the bride, the voice of those who will say:
'Praise the LORD of hosts,
For the LORD is good,
For His mercy endures forever' —
and of *those who will bring the sacrifice of praise into the house of the* LORD. For I will cause the captives of the land to return as at the first," says the LORD. (Jer. 33:10–11 NKJV, emphasis added)

The Hebrew word *todah* is translated "sacrifice of praise" in Jeremiah 33:11. It can mean thanks, thanksgiving, praise, and adoration. It comes from the Hebrew verb *yadah*, meaning "to give thanks or to give praise." The root of *yadah* is *yad*, which literally means "hand." This word meaning gives a picture of lifting or extending your hands in thanks toward the Lord God.

What God is saying here to Jeremiah is that the "sacrifice of praise" was not only worth mentioning, but was important enough to God that He makes a promise that its activity will be restored once He brings the captives back to the land He promised them. God obviously missed those sacrifices of praise and longed to hear them again from the hearts of His people.

> *You and I are to allow His praise to be continually on our lips, not because we have to but because we want to and we need to. God loves a sacrifice of praise!*

Another way to look at this is taken from the Psalms: "May *my prayer* be set before You *as incense*, the *raising of my hands* as *the evening offering* [sacrifice]" (Ps. 141:2, emphasis added). David, writing under the direction of the Holy Spirit, gives us a glimpse of what is to come under the New Covenant. Under the Old Covenant, incense was burned before the Lord continually and two lambs were slain each day as sacrifices for sin: a morning and evening sacrifice.

However, David sees down through the ages to where spiritual worship would one day replace physical offerings and take on an even deeper and more personal meaning. Each individual would now be able to offer spiritual sacrifices and offerings to God directly, without the aid of an earthly priest—because Jesus, the Messiah, has become our Great High Priest. Thus our prayers and the raising of our hands become part of our spiritual litany that we offer up to God individually, and collectively as the church—His body.

"Therefore, through Him [Jesus] let us continually offer up to God a sacrifice of praise, that is, the fruit of our lips that confess His name" (Heb. 13:15). Here we see yet another dramatic insight into our topic, "a sacrifice of praise." The writer of Hebrews tells us that we are to "continually offer up to God a sacrifice of praise." Continually, without cessation, you and I are at all times to praise and bless His name and give Him the glory that He so richly deserves. Our sacrifice is our speech, "the fruit of our lips." You and I are to allow His praise to be continually on our lips, not because we have to but because we want to and we need to. God loves a sacrifice of praise.

The Sweetest Praise

I believe that there is yet another reason that the sacrifice of praise is so treasured by the Lord. In fact, I think it must be to Him the sweetest praise of all because many times it emanates from a heart that has been crushed beneath life's difficulties. This kind of sacrifice comes with a price—a great cost, the value of which no one else but the worshiper and God know.

It takes the crushing of tens of thousands of flower petals to yield but an ounce of perfume. However, there is nothing in the world like the scent that is released through that crushing process, and perfume prices reflect that. When we are being crushed through circumstances and trials, and yet find it within ourselves by the power of the Holy Spirit to offer up a sacrifice of praise to God, the fruit of our lips becomes a most costly perfume to the Lord, released under the pressure of what we are going through.

There are times when we as believers in Christ Jesus undergo great trouble and turmoil, and at times it seems there is no way out. Have you ever been there? In the South, people like to say, "We'll be there, Lord willing and the creek don't rise." But what happens when the Lord isn't willing yet and the creek *is* rising? Then what are we supposed to do?

King David had high highs and very low lows, and his psalms reflect that. One minute he's a great man of faith and power, extolling the wonderful works of our God, and the next minute he's begging God to get him out of trouble. Sound familiar? It sounds like my life, and you are probably thinking it sounds like your life too. That's life—full of ups and downs, days when there's sunshine and days when there's rain.

Enemies Everywhere

Psalm 69 teaches us that even in the crushing challenges of life, we should offer up that sweetest of offerings to the Lord—a sacrifice of praise.
Save me, God,
for the water has risen to my neck.
I have sunk in deep mud, and there is no footing;
I have come into deep waters,
and a flood sweeps over me.
I am weary from my crying;
my throat is parched.
My eyes fail, looking for my God.
Those who hate me without cause
are more numerous than the hairs of my head;
my deceitful enemies, who would destroy me,
    are powerful.
Though I did not steal, I must repay. . . .
For I have endured insults because of You,
and shame has covered my face.
I have become a stranger to my brothers
and a foreigner to my mother's sons
because zeal for Your house has consumed me,
and the insults of those who insult You
have fallen on me. . . .
Rescue me from the miry mud; don't let me sink.

Let me be rescued from those who hate me,
and from the deep waters.
Don't let the floodwaters sweep over me
or the deep swallow me up;
don't let the Pit close its mouth over me. . . .
You know the insults I endure—
my shame and disgrace.
You are aware of all my adversaries.
Insults have broken my heart,
and I am in despair.
I waited for sympathy,
but there was none;
for comforters, but found no one.
(Ps. 69:1–4; 7–9; 14–15; 19–20, emphasis added)

This is gut wrenching and familiar territory to us because
we all have experienced at least some of what David is
expressing in this psalm. For instance, have you ever had
anyone hate you without a cause? It can be especially painful
when someone you know entertains a piece of gossip about
you, and instead of defending you, not only listens but also
believes it. Or when people misunderstand something you
did or said, and instead of coming to you, they try you,
judge you, convict you, and sentence you all by themselves.
Thankfully, God is our judge and not other people.

Then there are those moments we have all had when
enemies seem to come out of nowhere—we don't even see
them coming. They suddenly show up at work, at home, or
on the job. Enemies show up suddenly in the forms of sickness, fear, doubt, depression, and oppression. Like David,
we have enemies everywhere around us, and there are times
in our lives where we suffer because of their attacks. We can
feel the effect that they are having on us and we begin to cry
out to God for help.

Crying out to God is the proper response for every believer. We cry out to God to vindicate us against their accusation. We cry out to God to deliver us from the traps the enemy has laid. We cry out to God to lift us up and out of the deluge that's about to take us under, when we feel like we can't go another day. And if that's not bad enough, verse 4 of Psalm 69 says that there are times when we have to pay back what we did not steal. That has to be one of the bitterest pills to swallow—being accused of stealing and having to restore things that you never took.

> Crying out to God is the proper response for every believer.

Does any of this sound familiar? How many times have these kinds of things happened to you? What about when someone stole away a relationship from you and you had to do the work to get it back? What about the times when someone stole your joy away without a second thought and you had to go and get it back by yourself? What about when someone stole your reputation with someone you loved and respected and you had to go back and build it up again? How about when someone stole your dignity with belittling words and you had to pray for God to build your self-worth up again?

How many times have you had to restore something that was not your fault? It gets dumped into your lap somehow and you become responsible for the whole mess. Everyone around you just assumes you're responsible for the mess because they don't know the whole story—and maybe don't even care. Deep inside, you feel crushed and overwhelmed, and only God knows how you feel.

Verse 20 says, "Insults have broken my heart, and I am in despair." The word translated *despair* means "sickness" in Hebrew. Don't we all feel sick to our stomachs when someone has betrayed us or turned against us? That verse also says, "I waited for sympathy, but there was none; for comforters, but found no one." When you have that feeling of not having a friend in the world, and yet you've done everything that you know to do to live right for the Lord, what can you do?

It's Called a Sacrifice Because It Is

Through the years, different people have said to me, "What should I do after I have prayed, and attended church, and tithed, and worshiped, and given, and served, and quoted the Word, and believed—and things still aren't any better?" How should we respond when nothing has changed surrounding our circumstances? What should our response be? I would humbly submit to you—from my own experience— that our best response is yet another sacrifice.

After giving and giving and giving, we need to give again. We need to sacrifice again. This time, this most important of all times, we need to offer up a sacrifice of praise that is unlike anything else we have ever offered up. We must offer a sacrifice of praise to the Lord.

> *After giving and giving and giving, we need to give again. We need to sacrifice again.*

God knows it's a sacrifice to say "Thank you, Jesus" when nothing has changed. He knows it's a sacrifice to say "Hallelujah" when you are barely making it. He knows it's a sacrifice to say "Praise the Lord" when you can hardly say anything at all. He knows it's a sacrifice to say "Glory to God" when it seems you've lost more than you've gained. It is a sacrifice. It costs you something when you say these things. Those words you speak to Him have come at a price—but the beauty in it all is that you have chosen to go ahead and praise Him anyway.

Nothing is sweeter, nothing is more precious, and nothing is dearer to His heart than when you and I are offering up a sacrifice of praise. He gave up the blood of goats and bulls just to hear you and me praise Him, just to hear you and me tell Him that we love Him, just to hear you and me calling on His great name. It *is* a sacrifice. Even though we'd rather be quiet, or complain, or continue to talk about our mistreatment at the hands of others, we learn that those responses will get us nowhere.

After we have poured it all out before the Lord, after we have voiced our concerns, complaints, and petitions, we need to offer up a sacrifice of praise to Him just like David did:

But as for me—poor and in pain—
let your salvation protect me, God.
I will praise God's name with song
and exalt Him with thanksgiving.
That will please the LORD more than an ox,
more than a bull with horns and hooves.
The humble will see it and rejoice.
You who seek God, take heart!
For the LORD listens to the needy
and does not despise
His own who are prisoners.
(Ps. 69:29–33, emphasis added)

When we "don't feel like it," when we aren't even sure of ourselves anymore, when we feel like we're going under, when we know the battle is far from over—that's when we offer up a sacrifice of praise. God loves a sacrifice of praise because when it is offered up by His child He sees the core of a worshiper destitute without Him. Our hearts are laid out before Him when we are lifting up that sacrifice of praise. The only way out of our difficult situations is to go through them with hands raised and His praise on our lips.

"Therefore, through Him [Jesus] let us continually offer up to God a sacrifice of praise, that is, the fruit of our lips that confess His name" (Heb. 13:15). When I have to restore what I did not steal, I will offer up a sacrifice of praise. When I have been falsely accused, instead of answering the charges of the enemy I will offer up a sacrifice of praise. When people have misunderstood me, when so-called friends have taken out their frustrations on me, when I am given a medical report that is not good, when I have lost my job, I will still offer up a sacrifice of praise. When tears run down my cheeks at night and no one knows my private pain, I will offer up a sacrifice of praise.

> *Nothing is sweeter, nothing is more precious, and nothing is dearer to His heart than when you and I are offering up a sacrifice of praise.*

We are to offer it up "continually" because God inhabits our praise, and His wonders to perform attend His healing presence. No matter what you're going through, it's not over. God will have the last say.

God Is an Escape Artist

The reason that I can offer up a sacrifice of praise is not because I always feel like it. It isn't because I'm trying to be super-spiritual. It is because I have been through tough stuff before and I am still here. Somehow, some way, when I thought I would have lost my mind, when I thought I was about washed up, when I thought I was going under, when I thought I was done for, God made a way where there was no way.

That's why David praises Him after his laundry list of injustices, hurts, and complaints. God had delivered David before and David knew He would do it again. And what God has done for David He will do for you right now. God will bring you out.

When the devil thinks he has you cornered, God will open the secret door. The devil may box you in, but he can't put the lid down on you. God will open up a trap door beneath your feet and slip you out. God is an escape artist. "Our God is a God of salvation, and escape from death belongs to the Lord GOD" (Ps. 68:20).

He will make a way out for you. He will open a secret door. "No temptation has overtaken you except what is common to humanity. God is faithful and He will not allow you to be tempted beyond what you are able, but with the temptation *He will also provide a way of escape*, so that you are able to bear it" (1 Cor. 10:13, emphasis added).

> *No matter what difficulty you may face, attached to it is an exit sign!*

This is an awesome truth: No matter what difficulty you may face, attached to it is an exit sign. In other words, every room of test and trial that you enter will have an exit. Of course, we don't always realize that because not all exits are clearly marked. The devil will do everything he can to keep you from seeing the exit. He will lie to you, create a disturbance, try to cloud your thinking—he will do anything he can to keep you from seeing the exit. He knows that the exit is there because even he knows that God has promised it to His children.

I have discovered that when you're going through something tough, when you're going through the worst of times, when everything is breaking loose against you, there is only one way to find the exit: *Praise Him!* Praise will illuminate the exit. Praise will light up the room and scatter the darkness. Praise will cause you to see the light at the end of the tunnel. A sacrifice of praise—the fruit of our lips. Praise your way out the valley. Praise your way out of that difficult time. God's got you covered.

"You let men ride over our heads; we went through fire and water, but You brought us out to abundance" (Ps. 66:12). I may be all wet and smell like smoke when God gets me out of the fire, but I'll still be alive and I will still be offering up a sacrifice of praise. He will bring me out to a place of abundance. I will offer up praise before, during, and after my situation. Continually will I extol His greatness!

> God arises. His enemies scatter,
>> and those who hate Him flee from His presence.
> As smoke is blown away,
>> so You blow [them] away.
> As wax melts before the fire,
>> so the wicked are destroyed before God.
> *But the righteous are glad;*
>> they rejoice before God and celebrate with joy.
> *Sing to God! Sing praises to His name.*
>> *Exalt Him* who rides on the clouds—
>> His name is Yahweh—and *rejoice before Him.*
> (Ps. 68:1–4, emphasis added)

To Sacrifice Means to Kill Something

As I said earlier, God will have the last say. I know that in life we all face times that seem so uncertain, but take heart—go ahead and lift your hands to the Lord and offer up a sacrifice of praise. Pour your speech out before Him and watch the enemy scatter. God is moved by the heartfelt cries of His children, and He responds.

No sweeter smell ascends to His throne than the praise that is released through the crushing of difficult circumstances. While it is offered freely, it comes at a price and says, "I don't like what I'm going through, but I love and trust You and my confidence is in You, Lord! I know that Your deliverance is sure." There is something very freeing about that. Not easy, but freeing.

The word *sacrifice* means to kill or slaughter something on purpose. A sacrifice of praise slays our pride, our fear, our will, and anything that would seek to deter us from our worship of Jesus Christ. While our praise in the natural is a living sacrifice, in the supernatural it slaughters the things that destroy us from the inside out. We can make such a sacrifice with full assurance because we know that the power within any sacrifice of praise comes from Jesus Christ, who through His blood secured our salvation and provides ongoing cleansing.

> *A sacrifice of praise slays our pride, our fear, our will, and anything that would seek to deter us from our worship of Jesus Christ.*

As we "continually" offer up these sacrifices of praise, we are at the same time drawing closer and closer to God. We are laying an axe to the root of those things that want to lodge in our minds and hearts and keep us in inner turmoil. The "fruit of our lips" is important as well because as much as God longs to hear our praise we need to hear ourselves praising and honoring Him. Praise has a profound impact on our minds, wills, and emotions. Furthermore, it dismantles the lies of the enemy, which come like arrows dipped in pitch to inflame our minds. Our praise is a confession of our faith in God, and it becomes a mighty shield against those evil things.

*Don't stop praising Him — even in the hard times . . .
especially in the hard times. Instead, continually
offer up a sacrifice of praise.*

Part 3

Your Presence Is All I Need

Words & Music: David M. Edwards, Harlan Rogers, Caleb Quaye*

Verse 1:
Your presence is all I need
In your presence is where I want to be
Only your touch can satisfy me
Your presence is all I need

Chorus:
You are holy, holy, holy
Lord, God Almighty
Who was and is and is to come
You're above me, behind me
Right here beside me
Lord, your presence is all I need

Verse 2:
Your presence has ruined me
I've seen the glory of my chosen king
I lay down my life before your feet
Lord, your presence is all I need

Chorus:
You are holy, holy, holy
Lord, God Almighty
Who was and is and is to come
You're above me, behind me
Right here beside me
Lord, your presence is all I need

Chapter 7

The Way In

§ § §

*F*or years we have heard the terms *praise* and *worship* coupled together. I don't exactly know how that happened, but from childhood onward I have heard those two words together. Even the church bulletin reads "Praise and Worship Time." I've never seen it printed "Worship and Praise"—in fact, I don't think I've ever heard those two words used in that order. I'm not sure why they came to be linked as "praise and worship," but that order is certainly biblically accurate.

Praise sets the stage for worship. Praise is extolling God and thanking God for what He has done, is doing, and continues to do. Praise is telling of His wonderful acts and lifting His great name to the highest heavens. Praise is earth-shattering, ground-shaking, hand clapping, feet dancing, trumpets blaring, bell ringing, exuberant, exalting, extolling, and exciting. No wonder many of our corporate gatherings begin with a song of praise that sets the tone for what's about to take place. It anticipates what is to come: His manifest presence.

Entering His Presence

Shout triumphantly to the LORD, all the earth.
Serve the LORD with gladness;
come before Him with joyful songs.
Acknowledge that the LORD is God.
He made us, and we are His—
His people, the sheep of His pasture.
Enter His gates with thanksgiving
and His courts with praise.
Give thanks to Him and praise His name.
For the LORD is good, and His love is eternal;
His faithfulness endures through all generations.
(Ps. 100:1–5, emphasis added)

Enter through the gates to His presence with thanksgiving and move into the courts of the Lord with a gift of praise. It is inappropriate for us to barge into God's holy presence without praise on our lips and in our hearts. He is the Sovereign of the universe. We should come singing, shouting, dancing, praising, as we are told in His Word. He is willing to meet us anywhere, anytime, and anyplace, but we need to come into His presence with the praise and thanksgiving that He deserves and is worthy of.

> Praise sets the stage for worship.

Here on earth we have people who are willing to wait in line for hours for one glimpse of some earthly monarch or celebrity—yet we think nothing of running here and there through our week without ever accessing the King's presence on purpose.

Several years ago my wife and I had spent the day in Evian, France, and were headed back to Bern, Switzerland, for an evening of ministry. We crossed Lac Léman and disembarked at Lausanne to catch a train. When we got off the boat, there were huge crowds of people everywhere. It was not tourist season and the weather wasn't all that great, so we were curious as to why all these people had gathered near the dock. When we saw the press arrive, we decided to move closer to the barricade to see what was going on. A long, red carpet stretched from the curb through a park and to a huge yacht, and it seemed that we were waiting for someone.

> *It is inappropriate for us to barge into God's holy presence without praise on our lips and in our hearts. He is the Sovereign of the universe. We should come singing, shouting, dancing, praising, as we are told in His Word!*

We knew the Swiss had no monarchy, so who could this be? I asked around and the people told me that Queen Beatrix of the Netherlands was coming to board the royal yacht and sail to another port. I had never heard of Queen Beatrix but figured this would be kind of neat to see a real live queen. From the looks of everything, she was only minutes away—what timing.

We could hardly believe all the people who were involved in the preparations for her appearance. Secret Service-types were everywhere, helicopters hovered overhead; police, police, and more police; bomb-sniffing dogs, trumpet players, band members, and little guys in tuxedos standing by with a Bissell to clean up every falling leaf that landed on the red carpet. This was a well-oiled machine for sure. A few minutes soon turned into forty-five minutes and then an hour. We had about forty-five minutes left to catch our train and we still had to walk a ways to the station. But this was a chance of a lifetime, right? We decided we could wait a few more minutes.

Just when we were about to give up, a large caravan of limousines came down the street and parked along the curb. Every time someone got out, I'd ask anyone who'd listen to me, "Is that her?" After at least five or six carloads of what looked like very important people got out, everything stopped. No one moved. The trumpets started to play and then we heard someone very official shout: "Her Majesty, Beatrix Wilhelmina Armgard of Orange-Nassau, Queen of the Netherlands!" And out of the limo she came, big black feathery hat and all. People were going crazy and screaming, "La longue vie à la reine!" It was starting to get exciting.

The queen came down the red carpet, plumes from her hat blowing in the breeze, the little guys in tuxes looking for errant leaves, people yelling and cheering—it was pandemonium. She looked right at my camera, and I snapped that thing so fast that I was able to take another picture. She was regal, elegant, and classy. When she reached the water's edge, the band played the Dutch national anthem and everyone looked very solemn. I tried to look solemn too, since she was a queen. As soon as the band played the last note, some important-looking guy gave her a big parchment, the trumpets played, she boarded the yacht, and it was over. I looked at my watch—it had taken all of ten minutes for the entire event to take place. We waited over an hour for a ten-minute "audience" with a queen—from behind a barricade.

My wife and I laughed all the way back to Bern. Later that night as I was speaking at a worship event, God told me to tell the people what had happened that day at the water's edge, waiting for that earthly sovereign. I did. Then He told me to tell them this: "You will never have to wait in line for My presence. There are no barricades set up to keep you away or hold you back. The only barricade will be the barricade of your own will. All are welcome. Come now into My presence."

We were all in tears as the Spirit of God filled that place and the power of God began to move on the hearts of those European young people that knew far more about kings and queens than I did. They took to heart what I shared and responded to God's gentle call.

We live in a society that has devalued social graces and respect for others. Everything we do has become rush, rush, rush, run here, hurry there, and it has affected our treatment of the presence of the Holy! We think we can ramrod into God's presence, get a quick filler-up, and get on the road. And that is all a lot of people want.

Many believers do not understand that there is a spiritual protocol for every believer who wants to enter into the presence of the King. Praise is only the primer. Praise sets the stage for His entrance into our midst. Praise opens the way for worship to take place. The whole time we are praising, whether individually or corporately, the Holy Spirit is using that praise to whittle away at what's wrong on the inside of us. While we are praising God, the Holy Spirit is preparing our hearts for something far greater: worship and the Word.

The imagery in Psalm 100 presents a model for us to follow. It presupposes that those reading it or hearing it know well the tabernacle plan or the temple complex, and the entire sacrificial system of old. These illustrate how praise precedes worship. Praise is the way into worship, and worship is the way into an encounter with the living God. With triumphant shouts and thankful hearts, we make our way past the gates. Joyful songs and gladness bring us into the courts just outside the Holy Place. Then worship, prompted by the Holy Spirit, moves our hearts into that Holy Place where we begin to see and feel our great need of Him, His healing touch, and His saving grace. It is there in the Holy of Holies—not made by human hands—where God speaks to our hearts by His Spirit, reminding us of His promises and His deep, deep love for us.

I truly believe that people would be better equipped spiritually to face life's challenges and changes if they spent more time in God's Word and more time in worship. Worship is true communion with God. Worship is where we are "peaced" together.

We all have mental images of what a worshiper looks like. We each have our own ideas of what shape or form worship takes. I believe the best way into God's presence is to come broken, humble, and spilled out before Him. And to come with a gift—not a tangible thing, though the Lord may require that from us, but specifically the gift of yourself. The gift of "all you have." The gift of "whatever the cost." The gift of "you." Proverbs 18:16 says, "A gift opens doors for a man and brings him before the great."

Broken and Spilled Out

The time was around AD 33. It was springtime in Palestine—to be exact, it was six days before Passover. Jesus, one week away from His crucifixion, came to the small village of Bethany on the outskirts of Jerusalem. There he spent an evening with some of His closest friends: Lazarus, Martha, and Mary, a brother and two sisters who were followers of our Lord. A week earlier, Lazarus had been sick and died, but Jesus had raised him to life again. What conversation they must have shared!

At some point following the evening meal, Mary brought out an alabaster box containing spikenard—wonderful, fragrant oil imported from India at great expense. In fact, the amount of oil that Mary had was worth a whole year's wages. She bowed before the Lord Jesus, broke the seal on the alabaster box, and poured out its contents over His feet. When she poured the oil onto His feet, it must have run in and around every groove and muscle of each foot. The oil would have flowed between His toes and under His heels to the soles of His feet, washing away the dirt, dust, and stench of earth. After anointing His feet, she wiped them with her hair. As she performed this act of sacrificial loving worship, the Bible says that the entire house was filled with the fragrance of the costly perfume (John 12:1–8).

Everything she had she poured out in loving surrender to the Lord. Nothing was too extravagant for the One who would so extravagantly give His life for others. Their home must have smelled like spikenard for days.

> Worship is where we are "peaced" together!

The Bible doesn't give a continuation of this story, but I wonder if it went something like this . . .

After the crucifixion, Lazarus, Martha, and Mary returned home, overcome with grief. They were absolutely sickened by what they had just witnessed on Golgotha. The bloodied body of their Lord, Savior, and best friend was placed in a tomb not unlike the one Lazarus had lain in a few weeks before. Their conversation was full of thoughts like, *Remember the time He healed that little girl? . . . Oh, I remember the time He was teaching in the field beside the brook. . . . I'll never forget His face when I ran out to meet Him the day He brought you back to life, Lazarus. . . .*" Amidst the memories and tears, Martha got up to make everyone something to eat as each returned to his or her own private thoughts. And then, there it was again: that smell . . . that fragrance, . . . that sweet perfume that still stained the floor wafting through the air, filling their senses.

It was the scent of worship, it was the perfume of sacrifice, it was the aroma of total submission, it was the fragrance of being broken and spilled out.

Oh, to have that fragrance in my house the whole year through. To have that fragrance permeate everything that I am about. To have that sweet perfume released in my life again and again as I fall at His feet and worship Him. Loving Jesus must be my first priority. I want to be broken and spilled out.

An Opportunity Almost Missed

Now you know that anytime you do something for the Lord, there'll always be someone hanging around to second-guess you, to judge you, to make fun of you, to make light of your service to the King. For Mary, that person was Judas. He protested immediately, complaining about the cost of her sacrifice—when all the time he was dipping into the till. Judas was complaining about the price of her worship, saying the perfume should be sold and the proceeds given to the poor, when he couldn't have cared less about the poor.

> *Service that will have no other opportunity takes preference over perpetual (ongoing) duties.*

Then Jesus said, "You always have the poor with you, but you do not always have Me" (John 12:8). Can you imagine if Mary had missed this opportunity? Had she been saving the precious oil for such a time as this? What if she had given in to the thought, *Oh, I don't feel like doing it now, I'll do it next week?* Of course, next week would have been too late.

When Jesus said, "You always have the poor with you, but you do not always have Me," what He meant was this: Service that will have no other opportunity takes preference over perpetual (ongoing) duties.

People often say, "Well, if you're going to do it, you'd better do it now." And that is what we must come to terms with spiritually. How many times have we missed out on an opportunity to worship the Lord because we were too busy doing other things? How many instances have there been when it was just the Lord and me, but I went off to do something else? How many worship services have I been in where the service wasn't in me?

We've all had too many lost opportunities to do something for God. Let me tell you, if you're going to do something, you'd better do it now.

The Lingering Fragrance
of a Poured-Out Life

Mark's Gospel records this same anointing of Jesus by Mary. But he recalls something especially significant about the event. Jesus said, "I assure you: Wherever the gospel is proclaimed in the whole world, what this woman has done will also be told in memory of her" (Mark 14:9).

Imagine, here we are today, talking about what happened in the home of Lazarus, Martha, and Mary two thousand years ago. Jesus was right. But even more important than the recorded history of the event itself is *the lingering effect of a poured-out life.*

The lingering effect of her poured-out life causes me to hunger for that same sacrificial kind of worship. Though I cannot smell the spikenard she used, I *can* smell the fragrance of worship. I smell the fragrance of sacrifice. I smell the fragrance of brokenness. I smell the perfume of a life that was poured out. I can smell the pleasing aroma of the posture of her heart that says *no cost is too great if it's for the Lord Jesus Christ.*

I am a sentimental person. I cherish fond memories of family and friends, and especially those in my family who have passed on and are now with the Lord. I had two wonderful grandmothers, both Christians who loved Jesus very much. Both of my grandmothers wore those winter coats that had the big fur collars. When either of them would hug me, my face would stick right in that fur collar, and it smelled like walking through a perfume factory. The compounded effect of years and years of spraying her favorite perfumes had collected and concentrated in that fur collar, and I got to smell it on every visit.

Though as a child I made fun of it, today whenever I catch a whiff of those perfumes or something similar, I smile as my mind runs back to my grandmas hugging me and my little face hidden within those big perfume-soaked fur collars. I love that fragrance. I wouldn't trade anything for that aroma. It has left an indelible imprint in my memory.

When someone dies, it is not odd to pick up an article of clothing or some personal effect and notice the loved one's "smell" on it. Their perfume or cologne is like something left behind to comfort you. Then there are flowers and foods and plants that remind us of happy memories. One whiff can transport us back in time to that happy moment. People who live broken and spilled-out lives do the same.

> *Sacrifice for the sake of Jesus will have a perpetual influence.*

Sacrifice for the sake of Jesus will have a perpetual influence. I want my children to smell the fragrance of what I have done and be influenced by it. I want to lay a godly foundation in my home that will influence my kids long after I'm gone. I want them to remember the fragrance of me being poured out before the Lord, the fragrant scent of worship, the fragrant perfume of sacrifice, the fragrant aroma of total submission, the "house-filling" fragrance of being broken and spilled out.

You will always have difficult times in your life, but rather than creating a stumbling block for your kids, you ought to get down on your hands and knees and break open the alabaster box and pour it all out before the Lord. Rather than become bitter, why don't you worship and become better? Rather than leave the stench of jealousy and hard-heartedness, why don't you leave the fresh fragrance of faithfulness?

Then when your kids are facing tough situations, the sweet fragrance of your poured-out life will come lingering back to influence them to keep doing the right thing. The fragrance of the family altar will come back, the fragrance of mom and dad praying will come back, the fragrance of mom and dad worshiping will come back. That's what the Bible means when it says, "Train up a child in the way he should go, and when he is old he will not depart from it" (Prov. 22:6 NKJV).

The way in is through brokenness. Psalm 51:17 says, "The sacrifice pleasing to God is a broken spirit. God, You will not despise a broken and humbled heart." The way in is through humbling ourselves before Him. The way in is through pouring our lives out before Him in loving surrender. We spend so much of our time trying to act like we have it all together. Why don't we go ahead and throw our hands up before Him and say right now, "God, without You I'm nothing. The only good in me is that which You have placed there. I worship you. Mold and make me into what You would have me to be." That's worship.

Your Ministry *to* Jesus Must Come before Your Ministry *for* Jesus

Lazarus, Martha, and Mary all loved Jesus very much, but only one of them anointed His feet. Only one of them spent a year's wages on her gift. Only one of them bowed at His feet. Lazarus sat beside Jesus at the table. Martha was busy in the kitchen and busied herself serving people. But only Mary bowed at His feet, broke the seal on the alabaster box, and poured out the oil. Why didn't Lazarus jump up and do the same? Why didn't Martha stop what she was doing and join Mary?

Here we have a picture of the church. There are many people willing to sit beside Jesus, trust in Him for their salvation, and do little else. Then there are those who are so busy doing church work they don't even have time to pray or read their Bible or stop to worship and spend time with the Lord? Then there are those who have discovered that your ministry *to* Jesus must come before your ministry *for* Jesus.

To be perfectly honest, I don't know what people have to give out if they're not taking it in. If you're not spending time bowing before Jesus, how can you stand before men? When was the last time you took a good look at His feet? When was the last time you lavished the Lord with your love? He is thrilled when you involve yourself in ministry—

> *Your ministry to Jesus must come before your ministry for Jesus!*

it's part of our spiritual responsibility and development as a believer—but He longs for you to just love on Him the way Mary did. No agenda, no laundry list, no ulterior motive—just loving Him. When was the last time you just got alone with Him and said, "God, I want you to know how much You mean to me," and then tell Him, even if it takes all day. How can you serve a God with Whom you share no relationship?

The strength to stand is found in pouring your life out at His feet. The strength to do great things for God, to shape nations and cities, is found in some willing vessel pouring his or her life out at the feet of Jesus. In loving surrender, we need to be willing to spend everything we have for one moment at His feet.

The cause is greater than the cost. I want to empty myself before Him. When people are around me, I want them to be able to say, "I know that smell—It's the fragrance of worship, it's the fragrance of sacrifice, it's the fragrance of total submission, it's the fragrant perfume of being broken and spilled out."

Jesus Was Broken and Spilled Out

Like Mary's gift, Jesus was broken and spilled out for you and me. Isaiah 53:12 says,
Therefore I will give Him the many as a portion,
and He will receive the mighty as spoil,

because He submitted Himself to death,
and was counted among the rebels;
yet He bore the sin of many
and interceded for the rebels.

I was one of the rebels who He made intercession for. I was one of the sinners who He poured out His soul unto death for. Jesus was broken and spilled out for you and me. He spilled His own blood on the cross to save us—and the lingering effects of His poured-out life are still saving people to this very day. The sweet fragrance of the bloodstained cross longs to fill the house within you. Open up your heart. Jesus said, "This is My body, which is given for you," and "This cup is the new covenant [established by] My blood" (Luke 22:19–20). He was broken and spilled out.

When I came to Jesus, I knelt on my knees to pray, and through the air there came a familiar fragrance. The fragrance that I had grown accustomed to from my parents and grandparents was now being released in my prayers, as tears ran down my cheeks and I surrendered to the One who loves me most.

I've been in a lot of different countries and a lot of different places, and I can tell you that the fragrance of a broken and spilled-out life is the same everywhere. It is an aroma that is pleasing to the Lord. It shows up wherever there are people who have decided that the cause is greater than the cost. It shows up when people realize that they're in the presence of the sovereign King, and they surrender to Him their all. It shows up when we fall down at His feet.

Every time we encounter the Lord in worship, that fragrant and familiar smell will come: the perfume of worship, the incense of surrender. May the sweet perfume that we lavish on the Lord Jesus Christ in our worship pour off of Him and stain this old earth with a fragrance that will draw "whosoever will" to His healing presence. I pray that it will linger in your house for a lifetime and beyond.

May we each live lives that are broken and spilled out and may each of our homes be filled with the perfume of the King. He is worthy to be worshiped. He is worthy to be exalted. He is worthy of all glory and honor.

I refuse to be satisfied with simply standing in the courts of praise when the blood of our King has opened the door to His chamber. The veil is torn in two and He bids us to come before His throne boldly. The aroma of who He is fills the air. The Holy Spirit is pointing the way. Let's go in.

Chapter 8

The Presence and the Presents

§ § §

Settling into my seat by the window, I braced myself for a long transcontinental flight. I hated being by the window because I always had to climb over people to go to the bathroom, but I resigned myself to my fate.

Somewhere over the Arizona desert, about an hour out of Los Angeles, the flight attendant announced that they would be coming through the cabin with a snack. I expected the customary pretzels, of course, so you can imagine my surprise when the flight attendant handed me a basket with grapes and crackers. I was thrilled, but I thought it was quite unusual—they must have had some leftovers from some previous European flight or gone to the farmers' market. I really wasn't hungry, and my mind was occupied with the concerts I was on my way to do, so I continued to focus on working on my set list and making notes.

Without thinking, I began popping the grapes into my mouth. Suddenly I was startled by what I thought was an audible voice: "This is My blood, shed for you." I turned around in my seat to see who said it, but the businessman beside me was busy eating. In a second, I was enveloped in God's presence and I began to weep uncontrollably. I began to tell the Lord how much I loved Him, how I needed Him so much, and that I wanted to please Him with my life. I immediately began to thank Jesus for the blood He shed for my sins. I asked Him to wash me in His precious blood and to cleanse and wash away anything that was not of Him.

> God is big enough to do things that we may never understand. He doesn't need our OK to move in whatever way He sees fit to move.

I kept looking out the window to have some kind of privacy, as my tears did not stop falling down my cheeks. I put the cracker to my lips and again the voice came and said, "This is My body, broken for you." My sobs became deeper as I was overwhelmed with His love for me. The businessman beside me was now leaning forward, trying to see if I was OK. I could taste my salty tears as they mingled with that cracker in my mouth. Those grapes became His blood that day and those crackers became His body broken. Communion at thirty thousand feet! I was undone. I was a mess. God's powerful presence was simply wiping me out on this airplane as I sat in my seat beside the window.

God knew that morning before I ever boarded that plane that He would meet me there in that airplane. He had it planned all along. I didn't know it, but He did. That little seat against the window that I complained and mumbled about became the place of His presence. He made sure that grapes and crackers were on the menu. The Lord showed up there that day in such a powerful and special way. I will never forget that encounter with Him.

Later, as I made my way off the plane and waited at the baggage claim area, people kept looking at me as tears continued to fall. I was a bit embarrassed, but I couldn't help it—I had never experienced anything like this before. I was unable to suppress my emotions as wave after wave of God's glory came over me. I'm fortunate the rental car people gave me my car.

I really don't know how to properly explain what happened that day—not that I think I have to—but we always try to put these things into words to make it more understandable for others. Over and over in the Bible and in the history of the church, things that are simply unexplainable happened when God showed up, and our feeble attempts to explain them fall short.

God is big enough to do things that we may never understand. He doesn't need our OK to move in whatever way He sees fit to move. God is not concerned about any theological box people may have put Him in because He's really good at breaking the box. God is God, and besides Him, there is no other. We need to let Him be God and expect the unexpected when His presence shows up.

Living in the Place of His Presence

I want to live in such a way that I am always open to encounters with the Lord and that being in His presence becomes the most important part of my life. I want to live in the place of His presence—that is, any place where God lets down the ladder of His grace, blessing, mercy, and love. There we discover the supernatural connection between heaven and earth, between the temporal and the eternal, between the finite and the infinite, between the now and the not yet. After such a discovery, our hearts are moved to worship the Lord God with our whole being, giving Him the honor that He deserves. There, in "the place of His presence," we can build an altar upon which we must offer our very lives to Him in loving worship and surrender.

One of my favorite passages of Scripture to illustrate this is Genesis 28:1–22, where God meets Jacob at Beth-El. Here God's holy presence shows up unexpectedly and a connection is made between the temporal and the eternal, forever changing Jacob. Let's take a closer look at the latter half of that chapter:

Jacob left Beer-sheba and went toward Haran. He reached a certain place and spent the night there because the sun had set. He took one of the stones from the place, put it there at his head, and lay down in that place. And he dreamed: A stairway was set on the ground with its top reaching heaven, and God's angels were going up and down on it. The LORD was standing there beside him, saying, "I am the LORD, the God of your father Abraham and the God of Isaac. I will give you and your offspring the land that you are now sleeping on. Your offspring will be like the dust of the earth, and you will spread out toward the west, the east, the north, and the south. All the peoples on earth will be blessed through you and your offspring. Look, I am with you and will watch over you wherever you go. I will bring you back to this land, for I will not leave you until I have done what I have promised you."

When Jacob awoke from his sleep, he said, "Surely the LORD is in this place, and I did not know it." He was afraid and said, "What an awesome place this is! This is none other than the house of God. This is the gate of heaven."

Early in the morning Jacob took the stone that was near his head and set it up as a marker [altar]. He poured oil on top of it and named the place Bethel, though previously the city was named Luz. Then Jacob made a vow: "If God will be with me and watch over me on this journey, if He provides me with food to eat and clothing to wear, and if I return safely to my father's house, then the LORD will be my God. *This stone that I have set up as a marker [altar] will be God's house, and I will give to You a tenth of all that You give me.*" (Gen. 28:10–22, emphasis added)

Here is a story of a man who lived in the place of God's presence. Jacob had an exciting and unexpected encounter with God. What an unexpected revelation of God's presence and grace. What an unexpected discovery of the connection between heaven and earth. Jacob had a right response to God's revelation—he gave himself and his possessions to the Lord, in thankful recognition for God's favor and blessing. With God's blessing came the promise of His presence, guidance, and protection.

Eight Points of Understanding

With this text as our foundation and background, let us examine eight points of understanding for living in the place of God's presence.

1. In order to live in the place of His presence, you must follow God's directions

Following God's directions are paramount to living in God's presence. Jacob was following God's directions for his life. He was instructed, through his father Isaac, to go to Paddan-aram to find a wife. Jacob was heading in the right direction—he was right where he was supposed to be—and God showed up!

How many times have we not gone in the direction that the Lord instructed us to go? We not only missed His encounter and presence, but He was where we should have been, waiting for us to show up so that He could bless us and speak to us. How many encounters with God have we missed because we didn't follow directions and we never showed up at the right place and at the right time? God forgive us for not following directions. Directions—the Word of the Lord to us—are important! If we are ever going to live in the place of His presence, we are going to have to show up where He has called us to be. He will always call us to His presence—where there is fullness of joy and pleasures forevermore.

> *Jacob had a right response to God's revelation—he gave himself and his possessions in thankful recognition for God's favor and blessing!*

Jacob experienced God's presence because he was where he was supposed to be. Are you where you are supposed to be today? If not, move to where He is calling.

2. Living in the place of His presence, we learn that God's heavenly hosts are actively involved in our lives

Jacob's spiritual eyes were opened to the angelic involvement in his situation. The vision of angels suggests that they played an important part in God's protection and guidance of His people. Here, Jacob saw the connection between the earthly realm and the heavenly realm. Here, Jacob saw the intervention of the supernatural with the natural—the ordinary with the extraordinary. God was showing Jacob a glimpse of what is going on all the time—everywhere.

Under the New Covenant in Jesus' blood, angels are also active in the lives of believers, as well as in world events. They are continuously operating behind the scenes. Oh, if we could see right now in the supernatural realm, what a sight it would be! "Now to which of the angels has He ever said: Sit at My right hand until I make Your enemies Your footstool? Are they not all ministering spirits sent out to serve those who are going to inherit salvation?" (Heb. 1:13–14).

Whether you can physically see them or not, angels are constantly involved in the lives of the Redeemed: protecting, warring against the forces of evil, working in concert with the Holy Spirit to advance the ministry of Jesus and the building of His Church.

3. When we are living in the place of His presence, He speaks to us words of blessing and promise

God had been faithful to Jacob's father, Isaac, and his grandfather, Abraham. God had revealed Himself to both of them and now He would reveal Himself to Jacob in a most special way. God said, "I am the Lord"— in other words, "I am Jehovah, the self-existent One, the eternal One." After identifying Himself, God speaks blessing over Jacob about his future, and He promises to be with him and protect him.

> How many encounters with God have we missed because we didn't follow directions and we never showed up at the right place and at the right time?

When we are living in the place of God's presence, the Holy Spirit speaks to our hearts words of blessing and confidence about a wonderful future and an assurance of God's continued protection in our lives—if we continue to follow the way that leads us into His presence. The Lord is saying to us right now, "I will not leave you until I have done what I have promised you" (Gen. 28:15). "For you did not receive a spirit of slavery to fall back into fear, but you received the Spirit of adoption, by whom we cry out, 'Abba, Father!' The Spirit Himself testifies together with our spirit that we are God's children" (Rom. 8:15–16).

4. Recognize and celebrate the manifestation of His presence

After Jacob's encounter with the Living God, he said, "Surely the Lord is in this place." He recognized and then celebrated the event of God's presence. God wasn't interested in dwelling in some physical structure or geographical location—He was interested in being with Jacob. God is interested in being with His children. He is interested in being with you.

> When we are living in the place of God's presence, the Holy Spirit speaks to our hearts words of blessing and confidence about a wonderful future, and an assurance of God's continued protection in our lives—if we continue to follow the way that leads us into His presence.

God used the dream/vision to get Jacob's attention, but notice what the latter part of Genesis 28:16 says: "Surely the LORD is in this place, and I did not know it." "*And I did not know it.*" The significance of this statement is the fact that *God was there before the dream.* He was there all along. He'd been with Jacob every step of his journey. Jacob, however, was not spiritually "in tune" prior to this encounter. Again, it shows God's infinite mercy and love—to overshadow someone and look out for him or her even when that person doesn't fully know Him.

Aren't you glad that God watched out for you even before you were saved? Aren't you glad that God has been watching over you even in those times when you have not been spiritually "in tune"? Just because you don't *know* God is there doesn't mean that He's not. He's always there whether we *feel* Him or not! Thank God that reality is not governed by our feelings. His presence is not dependent upon our feelings.

I want to be so "in tune" with Jesus that I do not miss His presence. I want to be able to know and sense the presence of the Lord. I know that in His presence my spirit can breathe.

Surely the Lord is in any place where He's welcomed and worshiped. Remember, God knows no walls except the wall of our own wills. He will never force Himself into anyone's life. Let us welcome and expect His presence.

5. Anyplace where God lets down the ladder is a Beth-El

The ladder being let down was a sign to Jacob of God's activity in his life. When we open our hearts to the Lord, worship Him, pray to Him, and spend time with Him, He in turn lets down the ladder. This signifies two things: first, Jesus has opened a way of access to the Father—even the cross was a ladder of divine activity and intervention. The Lord can drop that ladder down at any time and at any place in your life where you need Him to be. Second, the activity on the ladder shows us that God is constantly at work in our lives.

> *Anywhere God lets down the ladder of His presence is a Beth-El.*

Jacob called this place where the ladder was let down, *Beth-El,* which means "house of God." Anywhere God lets down the ladder of His presence is a Beth-El. He brings the gate of heaven to your doorstep. We need more *Beth-Els* in our lives. Although the word *Beth-El* means "house of God," there was no house out on this desert plain. The house of God has nothing to do with a physical structure. The "house" is the canopy of His presence. And God desires to dwell in our hearts by His Holy Spirit. A *Beth-El* represents any place where God is present in a very special sense.

God knows where you are right now and He is more than able to reach you. You might feel like you are in the middle of nowhere, but remember that anywhere you are, He is. The very place you are *now* can become the gate of Heaven to your soul. The place you are *now* can become the dwelling place of God's presence if you will just let Him put His ladder down in the middle of your heart and allow Him to speak to you. Do it and you will say, "He is awesome in this place!"

6. Always build an altar

Jacob's response to his spiritual experience was to immediately build an altar. Our response should be the same. He built an altar, poured oil on top of it, signifying consecration (remember that oil is a symbol of the Holy Spirit), and then he made his vows to the Lord God Almighty.

When we have an encounter with the living God, we should build an altar unto Him. We need to mark the spot. We must not forget that as Christians it is our duty to remember what God has done and where He did it, and conversely we must recognize the danger of forgetting. You and I need to establish altars along our spiritual journeys. By doing so, we keep a record of our experiences with God. It gives us something to share with others about the importance of being faithful, and it encourages others by showing them how God has been faithful to us.

Our altars should serve as landmarks in our lives—points of remembrance that God intervened and let down a ladder of divine activity. At the altar we acknowledge His authority, sovereignty, dominion, and the fact that without Him we would be totally lost. After building the altar and pouring out the oil of consecration, like Jacob we need to apply action to our faith in God. We need to give ourselves to Him.

7. Always sacrifice

Altars are not made to look good; they're made to hold sacrifices. They are not supposed to be fancy things with nice coverings of fabric, holding objects of gold and silver. That kind of fancy altar leaves us with the wrong impression. Altars are made for killing things on. What good is it to build an altar every time you have an encounter with God, but never to sacrifice on those altars? Just like in a wedding, where vows are made before God and before the altar, we need to also make vows to the Lord at the altar as well—vows to love, honor, and obey God.

Jacob made a vow. He responded to God's presence with actions that showed God's rulership in his life and future. We must get up on top of our altar and slay whatever He asks of us in order to act out the fact that He is God, and besides Him there is no other.

I cannot help but see another aspect of giving in this text. Jacob vows to the Lord to give Him a tithe (a tenth) of all his income. This is important because it shows that he is following the godly example of his elders, but it is even more significant because it is before the giving of the Law and before God made it mandatory. This shows that Jacob knew that a proper response to God was to put God first in everything by giving Him a tenth of all of his increase. It also shows us that Jacob tithed, not because of some law, but because of his love for the Lord. We should tithe to the Lord, first and foremost, because we love Him and recognize that everything we have comes from Him to begin with. Second, we should tithe because we are encouraged to do so in His Word. The tithe is part of the Abrahamic Covenant of grace, not just the Mosaic Covenant of works.

This is why tithes and offerings are received in God's House—the church. The tithe is gathered (collected) in God's storehouse. It flows out of our worship to the Lord. How can we sing to Him and declare His praises and testify of His miracle-working power, and yet deny His authority in our finances and deny His ability to meet our needs?

Beyond his tithe, Jacob promised to serve the Lord for the rest of his life. We should give to God our very lives as living sacrifices. May we live in total submission to Him and His will.

8. In order to live in the place of His presence, we must live in a place of abiding

Abiding in Jesus requires time spent in His Word, time spent in prayer, time spent in worship, and most importantly, following His directions. We cannot live in the place of abiding and keep playing games with God. In order to get there, we have to be willing to leave wherever we are spiritually. In other words, we must leave the comfortable surroundings of our lukewarm commitment and walk into the passionate relationship with God that we so desperately need. We need to be close to His heart, next to His voice, and within the reach of His presence. Like Jacob, I'm more than willing to leave here in order to go there.

I thank God for the times that He shows up unexpectedly and surprises me. But there's something in me that urges me to expect Him to show up when I'm walking where He leads. There's an expectancy that a ladder of divine activity is going to be placed right in the middle of my situation. I want to live expectantly, anticipating His presence at every turn. Don't you?

Presence Produces Presents

Although in worship we do not seek God out just to get something in return, one cannot help but make the connection that His presence is followed by presents. Presents are unexpected blessings that God distributes just because He is God, and it is His nature to bless those who seek Him with their whole heart. God gives gifts to His children. Let me show you some Scriptures that illustrate what I'm talking about:

You reveal the path of life to me;
in Your presence is abundant joy;
in Your right hand are eternal pleasures. (Ps. 16:11)

God, Your faithful love is so valuable
that people take refuge in the shadow of Your wings.
They are filled from the abundance of Your house;
You let them drink from Your refreshing stream,
for with You is life's fountain.
In Your light we will see light. (Ps. 36:7–9)

Trust in the LORD and do what is good;
dwell in the land and live securely.
Take delight in the LORD,
and He will give you your heart's desires. (Ps. 37:3–4)

Blessed be the Lord,
Who daily loads us with benefits,
The God of our salvation! (Ps. 68:19 NKJV)

The presence of God is a holy thing. It is what makes an ordinary place extraordinary. It is what makes a natural gathering of people supernatural. His presence releases presents that are left in the wake of His "showing up" in our midst. That's why people are changed in the presence of Jehovah God. His presence stirs the Holy Spirit into operation, providing us direction for something specific or giving us His assurance and peace of mind. In His presence, the Holy Spirit confirms the truth of His Word, reveals and unfolds Scripture to us that sets us free, gives us His guidance, and crystallizes God's will.

All of these things are simply the result of His showing up. When God shows up in a place, His presence causes things to change. No wonder His Word tells us, "Everything is possible to the one who believes" (Mark 9:23). We must come to the point where we truly believe that any and all things are possible when God is present and actively involved in the situation. Goodness is God's very nature. Jesus told us that no one is good except God alone (Matt. 19:17). When He shows up, that attending goodness comes with Him and we are blessed in the process.

> We must leave the comfortable surroundings of our lukewarm commitment and walk into the passionate relationship with God that we so desperately need.

"Every generous act and every perfect gift is from above, coming down from the Father of lights; with Him there is no variation or shadow cast by turning" (James 1:17). God does not change; thus, what He did for Jacob He will gladly do for you and me. He loves you so much and longs to spend time with you. The "Beth-El" that you have been waiting for could be right there where you are, and you don't even realize it. His presence is all around you—honor it, bless it, and welcome it. God has something to reveal to you, so let Him.

I do not want God to show up somewhere where I'm supposed to be and find me missing in action. I want to be there when He calls and where He calls. I want Him to let down the ladder of His divine activity in my life. I want to recognize and celebrate the manifestation of His presence. I want to live in the place of His presence. Wherever He is, that's the place I want to be. I hope you feel that way, too.

Chapter 9

The Promise
of His Presence

§ § §

God has promised us in His Word that His presence will abide in any environment where He is welcomed — where He is worshiped. When God's people worship Him, there is a spiritually tangible presence that attends that worship. Something happens when we worship God. Our heartfelt praise invites Him to come and rule and reign in our lives and circumstances. Our praise becomes an entry point for God to move and establish His will in a situation. Praise brings a manifestation of God's presence because He has promised to show up when His children praise Him.

The Lord responds to our worship — whether it is corporate or individual. He shows up just as He promised. There is something about God's presence that is sensed and felt to a greater degree during a time of praise and worship than at any other time. Whether we are worshiping Him through the reading of His Word, or in prayer, or in song, His heart is moved by that, and in turn He responds; and when He responds we can feel it and know it.

Suppose you were to visit someone's house, and rather than ring the doorbell, you decided to just stand on the porch and wait for someone to open the door. You might wait for a couple of hours, a day, or a week. That door will not open until you ring the doorbell or knock, letting the people inside know you are there. When we praise God, we are ringing the doorbell, making our presence known, letting Him know that we have come to see Him. When He hears our praise, He gets up to open the door and invites us to come in. When we go inside, we move from praise to worship. In other words, praise is the vehicle into God's presence, and worship is what we do once we get into God's presence.

> *Praise is the vehicle into God's presence, and worship is what we do once we get into God's presence.*

We know that God is always home, so there's no worry that He's on vacation. We also know that we are always welcome at His place and that the doorbell is just protocol. But there's something about this holy protocol for us as individuals and as members of the Body of Christ. I think it must warm His heart to hear us gathering on the front porch to ring the bell because He knows we have come to spend time with Him on purpose. How privileged we are to be invited in for One-on-one communion.

God Manifests Himself in Worship

Psalm 22:3 says, "But You are holy, enthroned in the praises of Israel." While we know that God is everywhere (omnipresent), God is not *manifested* everywhere. God has chosen to manifest Himself in the praises and worship of His people. He is God Almighty, whose attending presence is revealed in a very real way when people worship Him. God is enthroned in our praises. Thus, our praise creates the atmosphere for an audience with the King.

Several years ago, Pastor Jack Hayford was referring to this verse when he said, "We do not manipulate God, but align ourselves with the great kingdom truth: His is the power, ours is the privilege and responsibility to welcome Him into our world—our private, present world."

We are not manipulating God as some would argue, we are simply acting on His Word and welcoming Him to come and have His away among us. He said that He is enthroned (seated) in the praises of His people.

When you or I go home from a day at the office or at work, we like to get comfortable. Most people want to have dinner, then kick back, sit down, and be "at home." It's hard to feel "at home" anywhere but our own home. We all have a place where we feel "at home" and where we can be ourselves. That's not to say that we're not ourselves on the job or at school, but we are more comfortable in a setting or an environment that is ours. Could it be that when God is enthroned in our praises, that's where He feels most at home? When you or I choose to make God at home through our praises, we are inviting Him to "act" at home. God obviously enjoys being seated comfortably in our praise.

> *Our praise creates the atmosphere for an audience with the King!*

Furthermore, something is bound to happen when we worship the Lord in spirit and in truth. I believe that something ought to happen when we worship Him because His very nature is to encamp and dwell among His people. I can't imagine God showing up and doing nothing, can you? When He's "at home" in praise, His heart is moved to speak, to heal, to comfort, to release. The Lord is not some idol that can be venerated—He is Jehovah God, whose presence is to be invited, welcomed, and expected. God has always been and is still "in the midst" of His people as they worship

Him. He responds to our praises, dwelling within them in such a way that we can sense it.

No doubt God would give up the worship of heaven's host of angels to come and be enthroned in your praise or mine! He would leave His throne in a second to hear you lifting up love and adoration to Him and in turn He would inhabit the very place where you are. He's already promised that He would move heaven and earth to meet your need every time you whisper His great name! Thus, why wouldn't He "show up" on the job, in your bedroom, at the office, in the park, and so on, if you'd speak His praise? He responds to our praises and dwells in them in such a way that we can sense it.

Some may think this just an emotional thing, but God created us—emotions and all. And though we may each sense His presence in a different way, unique to our make-up, the bottom line is that we can sense it and can walk away from a particular moment knowing that we've had an encounter with the living God. God lives in praise. God inhabits praise—anytime, anyplace, and anywhere. Praise is where God begins to make His presence known.

Whose Agenda Is It?

When I worship the Lord, whether on my own or in church, I come with an agenda: to meet with Him. And as important as that is, I need to remember that God has an agenda as well: to meet with me. Remember, *worship is all about relationship*. Of course, that's not to say that we don't have prayer concerns or needs on our hearts. But we have to learn the secret: if we seek Him first, all the rest falls into place. In seeking Him and making Him our first priority, He makes our needs His first priority. In His presence is "abundant joy," and at His right hand are "eternal pleasures" (Ps. 16:11). Fullness—completeness—is found in His presence.

As a worship leader, I need to stay sensitive to these principles as well. I need to remember that even more than we want to engage God He desires to meet with us. I've learned the hard way that the services in which we lacked the manifestation of His presence was because we weren't giving Him the time to speak and respond back to us during our times of worship. We were so busy following our "order of service" that we forgot to ask Him what His order of service was. After repenting, I remember saying, "Lord, what do You want to do?" Rather than staying satisfied with a brief visit with God, we began to hunger for Him to come and stay for awhile, and linger among us. We stopped being in a hurry and decided that since it's God's church, He should set the agenda.

> *If we seek Him first, all the rest falls into place.*

I think God would love to do more than visit us: He would love to camp out among His people. While we will always filter God's will through the grid of our humanness, we need to strive to "hear what the Spirit is saying" and what would be most pleasing to Him on each and every occasion. Since we have "this treasure" on the inside of our weak human vessels (2 Cor. 4:7), we need to allow that divine power to lead us in what is pleasing to Him when we gather to offer praise and worship.

I can hear people saying, "That's great, David, but we have three Sunday morning services, and if we're not out on time, it will affect the next service." I would respond, "It's what you do with the time you've got." Furthermore, when it comes to corporate gatherings, there could be other times set aside for people to gather together to worship God in some kind of extended format. But each of us can personally spend some one-on-One time loving on God and listening to Him. It is so important to our spiritual development to spend time in God's presence. Time—time in His Word, praying to Him, praising Him, and worshiping Him—is crucial to our relationship with Jesus Christ.

A Holy Equation

God does show up in the midst of His people's praise and worship. God inhabits, lives in, and is enthroned in our praise—it is His "home" element. Our praise and worship of the King of kings invites His presence to come. When God's presence shows up it is sensed, it is felt, and it is known. As that begins to take place, people begin to encounter God in a special way as the Holy Spirit manifests the presence of Jesus Christ. Let's look at the following holy equation:

Praise & Worship = His Presence

His Presence = An Encounter

Once people have encountered God's presence in worship, they will never forget it. There is nothing like the presence of God—there is no substitute for it in the universe. And once someone has encountered God in worship, it creates an insatiable desire for more of Him, and it deepens his or her love, respect, and awe of the Holy. What if more people were encountering God's healing holy presence in our churches? What would happen to this nation? What would happen to our world?

George Barna surveyed thousands of churchgoing Christians. The question was: "Have you ever experienced God in a worship service?" Only one-third said that they regularly experience God in church.[1] Not only is this tragic, but it tells us something else even more ominous: we are not leaving room for God to show up in our services. If people are not experiencing God in church, then it is no wonder our lives are lacking in power, understanding of our call, sense of mission, and clear direction.

We have the privilege of worshiping a God whom we can experience. If all we are doing is giving mental assent to our faith, we will find ourselves struggling spiritually. There is something about an experience that reinforces what you believe, and God knows that. He made us in such a way that we can each sense His presence when it shows up. Both individually and corporately, we need those spiritual times of refreshing that can only come from being in the presence of God. We need to walk away from them, as Jacob did, changed forever.

> *Once people have encountered God's presence in worship, they will never forget it.*

I cannot count how many times I have come into His presence spiritually dry and parched, with no breath left in me, and yet the rushing mighty wind of His Spirit has come to refresh and strengthen me. Encountering God is like a divine resuscitation of "holy oxygen" that fills our spiritual lungs anew every time we worship the Lord. As fresh morning air invigorates our physical lungs, so breathing in the presence of God in praise and worship invigorates us spiritually and helps to keep us spiritually fit for our calling and service to the King.

Again, we were created for a relationship with God, and the sum total of our response to Him in that relationship is our worship. Our worship is lived out in how we respond to God, His Word, and His will. We need to tear down every idol in our hearts until the only thing left standing is Jesus. One of the best ways to keep Jesus at the center of our lives is through worship—because as we come to Him in worship, the light of who He is illuminates every darkened corner of our souls and reveals the filth and dirt of our selfish ways, attitudes, and actions. There, exposed by the "Light of the World," we are without defense as we confess our sin and throw ourselves on His great mercy. What joy is ours when we find forgiveness and cleansing and draw closer to Him!

Jesus among Us

One of the most profound statements made by Jesus is found in Matthew 18:18–20. In the course of discussing church discipline and the believer's ability to bind and loose, Jesus reveals to us that His presence shows up when we are gathered in His name: "I assure you: Whatever you bind on earth is already bound in heaven, and whatever you loose on earth is already loosed in heaven. Again, I assure you: If two of you on earth agree about any matter that you pray for, it will be done for you by My Father in heaven. For where two or three are gathered together in My name, I am there among them" (Matt. 18:18–20).

> *Jesus must be the center of our worship and the object of our affection.*

Let's break that last sentence down and remember it's written in *red* . . .

- "gathered together"—a meeting
- "in My name"—an agenda
- "I am there among them"—a presence

Gathering in His name is the one activity of the church that we must never allow to get old, stale, dry, dead, or worn-out. The presence of Jesus is promised; however, we must come with an agenda that is "in His name." He is the purpose for gathering together—it's all about Him. He's the reason, He's the focus, and He's the gathering center. Jesus must be our audience of significance. We are to worship an audience of One. Jesus must be the center of our worship and the object of our affection.

When we gather together in His name, we should come expecting the breath of God not only to call us together as His body but to resuscitate us with the life-giving breath of His Holy Spirit. The promise of His presence is our reward every time we gather in His name. And when Jesus is present, everything is possible and available. Remember, in His presence is "abundant joy" (Ps. 16:11).

This promised "presence," remember, is a concentration of the essence of God—His glory. The Hebrew word for "glory" is *chabod*, meaning God's honor, God's renown, God's majesty, God's glory, and God's visible splendor. This same visible splendor filled Solomon's temple, and it will one day fill all the earth (1 Kings 8:11; Num. 14:21).

The presence of Jesus in the midst of two or more is a form of this same glory. Jesus joins us and helps us to escape the bondages of ourselves. Jesus' presence among us when we gather in His name is yet another proof of His deity. He does indeed show up when we gather to worship Him—and that's a promise.

It is this presence—this glory—that creates the right environment for an "encounter" with the living God. Whether it is the Holy Spirit gripping our hearts with conviction, or speaking God's Word to our spirits, or encouraging us to step out in faith, God's glory and presence are among us when we gather together in the name of His Son, Jesus Christ.

The Holy Spirit Active in Worship

Furthermore, the Holy Spirit works within each believer to do whatever He has to in order to awaken and deepen our awareness of and need for Jesus' presence in our lives. He does this by drawing our hearts closer to the Lord in our faith in God, in our love for God, our obedience to God, our communion with God, our hunger for God's Word, and in our praise and worship of God. It is "deep calling unto deep." The Holy Spirit—the deep in us—calling unto God—the deep in heaven. And the precious Holy Spirit draws us into the deep waters of worship where we can experience the presence of God within the veil.

I cannot emphasize enough the role of the Holy Spirit in our worship. His is the still small voice that encourages us to lift our hands in surrender, to praise Jesus with everything in us, to fall at His nail-scarred feet in worship. The Holy Spirit is constantly and consistently working within believers to deepen our experience and our walk with the Lord. He is the leader and guide to all truth and righteousness. He is the light within that illuminates God's Word and our understanding of it. If we will cooperate with His promptings, we will be taken to new places in our relationship with the Lord and in our times of worship.

> The Holy Spirit works within each believer to do whatever He has to in order to awaken and deepen our awareness of and need for Jesus' presence in our lives.

True worship is mouth-to-mouth resuscitation . . . deep calling unto deep. Worship is coming into His presence and allowing the life and power of God's Holy Spirit to fill our lungs (see Ezek. 37:1–14). The promise of His presence will work every time. And when Jesus is present, everything is possible and available. Can you imagine Jesus showing up without wanting to touch us, heal us, assure us, comfort us, release us, deliver us, save us, fill us? You see, in the atmosphere of God's presence, our faith is emboldened and it reaches up to receive what we need. Jesus said, "With God all things are possible" (Matt. 19:26).

True worship will always break down pride and fear. In true worship, pride must go because we must admit that we cannot do anything on our own to make it and we desperately need God's help, grace, mercy, and love. True worship confronts our fears because we are going to either have faith in God or give in to what we are afraid of. We realize that we cannot serve two masters.

Praise and worship build our faith as does reading and memorizing God's Word and quoting it aloud. This sends fear scurrying for cover. Fear is the enemy of faith. God's assurance that He will meet our needs and deliver us comes on the wings of worship. As we worship, He speaks back, and we leave that encounter encouraged and built up in our faith. Don't be afraid, God knows what He's doing. Put your trust in Him as you lift your praise and words of worship. Frederick Buechner declared, "God calls you to the place where your deep gladness and the world's deep hunger meet."[2]

> Fear is the enemy of faith!

In recent years, I have become more and more convinced of a strong sentiment that is pervading the Church: people are tired of being entertained, tired of seeing things hyped for an emotional response, tired of anything that seems fake or insincere. Why? People are hungry for the real power of the living God! People are hurting, and a church program that just gives a pat on the back isn't going to cut it. People need the power of God. One taste of God's presence will strike such a chord in the hearts of the hurting that they will not be able to replicate that taste anywhere else. All of the fullness that comes from being in God's presence makes everything else pale in comparison. There is no substitute for it.

God's presence is *not* predicated or predetermined by our feelings. God shows up no matter what we may feel like because He keeps His promises. The size of the crowd does not determine His willingness to show up, either.

Years ago, when we were planting a church, we started holding Wednesday evening worship services. Many times in those early days, I would look out from behind the stage at the crowd of three or four people and think, "Oh brother . . . why bother?" I would be in a sulky mood before I ever got to the keyboard. I would plow on through the services only to discover that God didn't care how many showed up; only I did. He was ready to meet with whoever had come.

Let us thank God that He has promised to enthrone and inhabit our praises and that Jesus has promised to show up when we gather together under the banner of His great name. Let us hold fast to these truths and move ahead with a fresh understanding that all things are possible when God shows up on the scene and that fullness of joy is found only in His presence.

Part 4

Breathe Your Name
Words & Music: David M. Edwards*

Verse 1:
When I've praised You for a thousand years
I will have only just begun
To give You all the glory and honor
That You're deserving of...

When I think about You, Lord,
And all that You have done
I cannot comprehend the vastness
Of Your never ending love...

Chorus:
And I breathe Your name
I breathe Your name
I breathe Your name, Jesus

Verse 2:
I used to think that You loved heaven
And loved sitting on Your throne
But through Your Word I've learned
There's another place that You would rather go

In the praises of Your people
Is where You'd rather be
Enthroned in loving adoration
From the ones that You've set free

Chorus:
And we breathe Your name
We breathe Your name
We breathe Your name, Jesus

Chapter 10

Throne Room Encounters

§ § §

Our praise "enthrones" the Lord, and as He is enthroned in that praise, it becomes a place where His presence abides. He takes up residence in our praise and worship—He is in our midst. I like to think of these times as "throne room encounters." That's because anywhere, anytime, and anyplace where God shows up becomes a sacred space—His sacred space—as He is seated in our praise. It is that sacred space that becomes like an invisible throne room where the King of kings is granting audiences.

From biblical times to the present day, monarchs have had a physical place where they sit on a throne. From there they make decisions on behalf of the people they rule, entertain dignitaries and guests, grant or deny requests made to them by their constituents, and permit audiences or visits from everyday folks who come and speak to their king or queen. More than one of these throne rooms was also called "The Presence Chamber" because when the monarch was seated, his or her "presence" or "face" was in that room.

Given what we know of our Lord and Savior through His Word, church history, and our own experiences, it's not much of a stretch to see how that kind of an earthly model relates to any believer having an audience with the King of kings. Though God does occupy and possess a very real throne in heaven, He also occupies His children's praises by His Spirit. Remember our formula?

Praise and Worship = His Presence

His Presence = Encounter

Those throne room encounters are worship experiences. They are connections made between heaven and earth—like something that bridges a horizon that divides earth from sky.

> *Some very significant things happen in a throne room. It is where the Majesty is seated, where audiences are granted, and where decisions are made!*

Throne room encounters are the "in between": the place that suddenly appears as we worship the Lord. God shows up, and the natural becomes infused with the supernatural. Those kinds of spiritual intersections leave us changed forever. How could they not? We need those times of spiritual refreshing where God pours out His Spirit on us as we abandon ourselves to Him in worship.

"You reveal the path of life to me; in Your presence is abundant joy; in Your right hand are eternal pleasures" (Ps. 16:11). In our worship, we are ushered via the Holy Spirit into God's throne room, i.e., His presence. Some very significant things happen in God's throne room. It is where the Majesty is seated, where audiences are granted, and where decisions are made.

With these things in mind, let's look at some throne room encounters that took place in the Bible and see what happened when God showed up.

Biblical Encounters

God's Word is packed with throne room encounters. It is especially enlightening to see the correlation between the individuals encountering God and the effect it had on their lives. Individuals, groups, and indeed history itself has benefited as a result of special encounters with God through worship. Biblical accounts of transformed lives increase our own hunger to experience the same. The following are only a few examples of what happened following a throne room encounter.

Isaiah's Encounter

In the year that King Uzziah died, I saw the Lord seated on a high and lofty throne, and His robe filled the temple. Seraphim were standing above Him; each one had six wings: with two he covered his face, with two he covered his feet, and with two he flew. And one called to another:

Holy, holy, holy is the LORD of Hosts;
His glory fills the whole earth.

The foundations of the doorways shook at the sound of their voices, and the temple was filled with smoke.

Then I said:

Woe is me, for I am ruined,
because I am a man of unclean lips
and live among a people of unclean lips,
[and] because my eyes have seen the King,
the LORD of Hosts.

Then one of the seraphim flew to me, and in his hand was a glowing coal that he had taken from the altar with tongs. He touched my mouth [with it] and said:

Now that this has touched your lips,
your wickedness is removed,
and your sin is atoned for.
Then I heard the voice of the LORD saying:
Who should I send?
Who will go for Us?
I said:
Here I am. Send me.
And He replied,
"Go! Say to these people: . . ." (Isa. 6:1–9)

Isaiah was commissioned to go and speak to his people only after he saw the Lord "seated on a high and lofty throne." Isaiah encountered the supernatural where he saw and heard angelic worship to God. He beheld the Lord in worship, listened to God's voice, and responded. Had he not entered into worship, he could have missed his destiny. When we worship, we become aware of our need for cleansing, and the blood of Jesus washes us clean as we confess our sin. When we worship, we also need to listen as God will often give us new direction or confirm His will through the heart promptings of the Holy Spirit. God is speaking . . . are you listening?

Throne room encounter result: Isaiah was cleansed, commissioned, and sent forth to minister.

The Eleven Disciples' Encounter

The 11 disciples traveled to Galilee, to the mountain where Jesus had directed them. *When they saw Him, they worshiped*, but some doubted. *Then Jesus came near and said* to them, "All authority has been given to Me in heaven and on earth. Go, therefore, and make disciples of all nations, baptizing them in the name of the Father and of the Son and of the Holy Spirit, teaching them to observe everything I have commanded you. And remember, I am with you always, to the end of the age. (Matt. 28:16–20, emphasis added)

The Great Commission was given after a worship encounter that the disciples had. I love the fact that the Scripture says simply, "When they saw Him, they worshiped." Shouldn't that be our response? When we see Jesus, we should worship. When we behold Him, we should worship. Undoubtedly, Jesus' heart was touched and moved by their worship. Again, we see that worship is a two-way street.

Jesus received their worship and then responded. The history of mankind was changed forever because Jesus' disciples were moved beyond themselves in a worship encounter. Their faith was fed, and they refused to allow anything to stop them. You and I and every other believer are living proof of the effect this worship encounter had on these men.

Throne room encounter result: The history of mankind was changed to this day—and continues forever—sweeping the globe with the Good News of Jesus Christ.

Day of Pentecost Encounter

When the day of Pentecost had arrived, *they were all together in one place.* Suddenly a sound like that of a violent rushing wind came from heaven, and it filled the whole house where they were staying. And tongues, like flames of fire that were divided, appeared to them and rested on each one of them. *Then they were all filled with the Holy Spirit* and began to speak in different languages, *as the Spirit gave them ability* for speech. (Acts 2:1–4, emphasis added)

The coming of the Holy Spirit on the Day of Pentecost came in the midst of a worship encounter as 120 followers of Jesus obeyed His command to remain and pray until the promised power came (Acts 1:4–7). Within minutes of this initial outpouring of the Holy Spirit, three thousand were saved and added to the church. As believers continue to be filled with the Holy Spirit's power, the preaching of the gospel with signs and wonders still spreads throughout the earth. The beauty of what happened here is that the 120 "were all together in one place." There was unity in their prayer and worship and focus.

> Worship is a verb—it is love in action.

Throne room encounter result: Three thousand people were saved.

Antioch Church Encounter

In the local church at Antioch there were prophets and teachers: Barnabas, Simeon who was called Niger, Lucius the Cyrenian, Manaen, a close friend of Herod the tetrarch, and Saul.

As they were ministering to the Lord and fasting, the Holy Spirit said, "Set apart for Me Barnabas and Saul for the work that I have called them to." Then, after they had fasted, prayed, and laid hands on them, they sent them off. (Acts 13:1–3, emphasis added)

The apostle Paul's first missionary journey was commissioned when the Holy Spirit spoke while they worshiped and ministered to the Lord. What is awesome about this is that we see the direct link between their worship ("ministering to the Lord") and God's responding to that worship ("the Holy Spirit said . . ."). The Greek word used here for "ministering" is *leitourgeo* from which we get our English word *liturgy.* The word used here is a verb. Worship is what we *do.* Worship is a verb—it is love in action. And God responded through a prophetic utterance and gave direction to the assembled worshipers. The glorious gospel of Jesus Christ was spread throughout Asia Minor and Europe as a result of a worship encounter. They stayed long enough to hear what God was saying.

Throne room encounter result: The spreading of the gospel to Asia Minor and beyond.

Philippian Jail Encounter

About midnight *Paul and Silas were praying and singing hymns to God, and the prisoners were listening to them.* Suddenly there was such a violent earthquake that the foundations of the jail were shaken, and immediately all the doors were opened, and everyone's chains came loose. When the jailer woke up and saw the doors of the prison open, he drew his sword and was going to kill himself, since he thought the prisoners had escaped.

But Paul called out in a loud voice, "Don't harm yourself, because all of us are here!"

Then the jailer called for lights, rushed in, and fell down trembling before Paul and Silas. *Then he escorted them out and said, "Sirs, what must I do to be saved?"*

So they said, "Believe on the Lord Jesus, and you will be saved—you and your household." Then they spoke the message of the Lord to him along with everyone in his house. He took them the same hour of the night and washed their wounds. Right away he and all his family were baptized. He brought them up into his house, set a meal before them, and rejoiced because he had believed God with his entire household. (Acts 16:25–34, emphasis added)

Paul and Silas were bound and shackled in a Philippian jail, put there on trumped up charges. Though bound in body, their spirits were free—free to worship. Somewhere around midnight, their unchained praise and worship began to touch the heart of Almighty God. And as they worshiped the Lord, He caused an earthquake to take place that not only shook the prison doors open but shook their chains off as well.

> *You can praise your way out of any prison if you know how to worship.*

We must also see in this passage of Scripture that our worship of the Holy has an effect on others as well. The other prisoners were listening to them. Like soothing ointment, their worship must have massaged itself into the hurting hearts of those other men bound in chains. How wonderful to hear such beautiful music in such a filthy and horrible place. Paul and Silas's praise could not be bound. You can praise your way out of any prison if you know how to worship. Then the jailer, this carnal man just doing his job, amazed at the secret these two possessed within, fell at their feet in hunger for what they had. What a sight!

Throne room encounter result: the Philippian jailer and his whole household received Jesus as Lord and Savior, and the other prisoners witnessed God's power.

Throne Room Encounters
Equal Great Things

Great things happen when we worship God: You might be in need of an earthquake to loose your prison doors—it starts with worship. You might need a clear call from God as to what direction you should take—it starts with worship. You might need God to pour out a fresh anointing on your life, commission you into a ministry, or release you into your destiny—it begins with worship.

We need to begin to praise our way up, out of, and into what and where God calls us to be. God loves us where we are, but He is calling us to move on. God's presence makes everything and anything possible to those who believe. When He shows up, nothing is impossible. His presence emboldens the troubled heart and strengthens the weary mind. His presence leaves an indelible image pressed deep within.

Our own throne room encounters will have a lasting effect on who we are and our understanding of who we are called to be. Furthermore, their effects will spill

> *God loves us where we are, but He is calling us to move on!*

over into the world we live in and onto those we come in contact with. There is a vital link between our "upreach" in worship and our outreach in evangelism. Let God pour out the oil and wine afresh and anew and take you to places you've never been.

One of the common threads that weaves its way through each of the worship encounters we've discussed is that the worship of the Lord came first and then the doing for the Lord followed. As we discussed earlier, ministering *to* the Lord must always come before ministering *for* the Lord. If we keep to that, our spiritual progress both personally and corporately will extend and expand beyond anything we ever dreamed.

"Worship is the goal of evangelism and evangelism is the fruit of worship."
—GERRIT GUSTAFSON[1]

Chapter 11

The Fruit of Our Own Throne Room Encounters

§ § §

A throne room encounter happens when we simply open our hearts in praise and worship to God and His presence shows up. These encounters are filled with God's power, which is dispensed and displayed in a multitude of ways. Thus, these worship times produce fruit in our lives. When we are exposed to the presence of God, things happen in us and through us. Fruit is borne in three main areas as the result of a believer spending time in God's presence: purity, purpose, and power.

Purity— We Are Changed in His Presence

In God's holy presence, we find the conviction of sin that must precede conversion, as well as encourage ongoing spiritual maintenance for believers.

But if we walk in the light as He Himself is in the light, we have fellowship with one another, and the blood of Jesus His Son cleanses us from all sin. If we say, "We have no sin," we are deceiving ourselves, and the truth is not in us. If we confess our sins, He is faithful and righteous to forgive us our sins and to cleanse us from all unrighteousness. If we say, "We have not sinned," we make Him a liar, and His word is not in us. (1 John 1:7–10)

John is addressing believers. He is teaching the church about the ongoing cleansing power of the blood of Jesus. It was and is powerful enough to save us and set us free and it was and is powerful enough to keep us by providing ongoing cleansing when we sin or make a mistake and need to be forgiven.

When I am worshiping the Lord through my prayer time, through singing, or through being in His Word, I am inviting Him to come and probe my heart to see if there is "any wicked way in me," so that I can confess it and draw closer to Him.

God never points out our sin simply to condemn us with it. By His Holy Spirit, He convicts us of the error of our ways so that we can confess those things that are binding us or holding us back from being who He's called and created us to be. We can live free from a guilty conscience. In worship, spiritual inventory is taken as the light of His holiness shines upon our lives.

On numerous occasions, whether in a public worship service or just worshiping the Lord at home, I have experienced the Lord pointing out to me areas where I need to confess sin. When I am worshiping, the closer I get to Him, the more I sense my need for Him and the deeper His light shines into the recesses of my heart. Things can surface that

I forgot were there. Issues can come to light that I thought were over. Becoming more like Jesus—this is true heart-holiness.

There is *no* condemnation for those who are in Christ Jesus, but there is conviction—and thank God for it. Instead of running from it, we should embrace it—the Refiner's holy fire. It's a good sign when you hear that still small voice say within, "You shouldn't have that attitude . . . you shouldn't have told that dirty joke . . . you shouldn't be holding on to that grudge." That is part of the Holy Spirit's role in our lives. He knows the mind of God and He is working in concert with the Father and Son to help us fulfill our destiny and purpose.

> *God never points out our sin to simply condemn us with it. By His Holy Spirit, He convicts us of the error of our ways so that we can confess those things that are binding us or holding us back from being who He's called and created us to be.*

For me, music is often the vehicle that the Lord will use to usher me into His presence. As I focus on Him and His attributes, His love for me, and Jesus' sacrifice for my sins, I realize anew and appreciate afresh the price that He paid and feel so ashamed of my selfishness and self-centered agenda. Broken and undone, I ask for His forgiveness once again and confess my inability to live a good and holy life on my own. This is what true worship will do in the heart of each of us. True worship will produce purity.

God's Word tells us that without holiness, no one will see the Lord (Heb. 12:14). I want to see not only the Lord in the beauty of His Holiness, but I want to see what the Lord is doing and be able to listen from a clean heart and a cleaned-out mind. In His presence the precious Holy Spirit points out our sin—not to condemn, but to spur us on toward full surrender by asking Jesus' forgiveness and pleading the merits of His blood so that we may be washed clean. Purity and a lifestyle of purity are essential in the life of a worshiper. We are changed in His presence.

Purpose— We Are Challenged in His Presence

In God's presence we receive direction. The throne room is where decisions are made and the battle plans are drawn. Jesus said that His Holy Spirit would take from what is His and make it known to us.

> "I still have many things to tell you, but you can't bear them now. When the Spirit of truth comes, He will guide you into all the truth. For He will not speak on His own, but He will speak whatever He hears. He will also declare to you what is to come. He will glorify Me, because He will take from what is Mine and declare it to you. Everything the Father has is Mine. This is why I told you that He takes from what is Mine and will declare it to you." (John 16:12–15)

Clearly Jesus is speaking here of the indwelling presence of the Holy Spirit within the believer. This is yet another fulfillment of the "type and shadow" experienced by those who served God under the Old Covenant. Just as Isaiah was told, "Go! Say . . ." only after he worshiped the Lord and had been in His presence, so you and I can receive clear direction from the Holy Spirit after we have worshiped in God's presence.

It is imperative and essential to know what God has *said*. But it is equally imperative and essential to know what God is *saying*. God has a lot to say about your and my situations. God has a lot to say that is applicable to our situations right now. Rather than supposing He's going to say and do the same thing in the same way He did last time, why don't we listen and linger long enough to get God's Word for the now—the *right now*. God is current, and while He has a positive track record in the life of each of us, He is bigger than having to duplicate or replicate what He said or did last time around.

We need the *rhema* of God. We need the fresh Word of the Lord. We need to get on our faces and seek Him until He comes and rains down His directives for our lives. Have you ever been in worship or prayer when the Holy Spirit brought to mind a Scripture that you would never have thought of on your own? That's a *rhema* word—a "*now* word."

> *When we draw near to God in worship, we discover what His heartbeat really is.*

True worship births now words. God responds and gives clear and concise directions. You might ask, how do I know that what I'm hearing is from God? First, it will always line up with His written Word. Something that is truly from the Spirit of the living God will always be in harmony with God's written Word. Remember, it was the Holy Spirit who wrote the Bible through the frailty of man. And second, it will always align itself with God's righteous and holy character.

When we draw near to God in worship, we discover what His heartbeat really is. His concern for the lost, lonely, and hurting is made known to us as He presses His heart against ours in our worship. He gives us direction for our personal lives and ministries as well. My own call to the ministry came in the middle of a worship time. I receive my clearest direction still when I am worshiping God. I can enter His presence confused and in doubt, and leave knowing what I am to do, or leave knowing that I am doing all that I'm supposed to do at that moment.

Prophetic vision for life and ministry often flows out of our times of worship. That shouldn't be a surprise to us. It's scriptural, it's practical, and it's God's nature to respond, lead, guide, and direct. I feel challenged when I've been in His presence. Challenged to follow His will. Challenged to pursue His will. Challenged to live His will. We are challenged in His presence.

Power—
We Are Charged in His Presence

In God's presence His power is displayed. The world is hungry for the manifestation of the power of God. People are healed in His presence. People can be healed during the worship service without any stop in the flow of things. God's presence is the most powerful thing in the universe. The gifts of the Holy Spirit are often very active during throne room encounters.

When unbelievers come in among God's people and the gifts of the Holy Spirit are in operation and God's presence is real in the room, 1 Corinthians 14:24–25 says that the unbelievers' untrained, immediate response (which is instinctive as well) is to fall down and worship God. Thus the power of God, which flows out of His presence, results in people receiving Christ Jesus as their Lord and Savior. Jesus said that if we lift Him up all men will be drawn to Him. "For the kingdom of God is not in talk but in power" (1 Cor. 4:20).

People can argue all they want about whether or not they believe in God's manifest power—but while they argue, God continues to manifest His miraculous power and the world continues to be manifestly in need of it. Only God's power can be the explanation for much of what I've seen through the years. I have seen the lame walk, the blind see, the deaf hear, the demonic set free, crippled limbs straighten, peace come to the mentally disturbed—all within the context of a "regular" worship service. This should be the norm, not the exception.

I have seen the power of God so real during a worship time that men and women went running to places of prayer screaming their confessions to God and asking for His mercy. I have seen people en masse, without any invitation, get up and move forward to pray at altar rails. I have seen hundreds fall under the power of God without anyone touching them or encouraging such behavior. All during "regular" worship. God is real and He is serious about meeting people's needs, whatever they may be.

> *When people are in the presence of God, the supernatural strikes a chord within the heart of every man and woman because we were created to worship Him and to respond to His presence.*

You see, when people are in the presence of God, the supernatural strikes a chord within the heart of every man and woman because we were created to worship Him and to respond to His presence. It feels right because this is what we were made for. Men and women find a connection made when God shows up. They may not even know what to call it because they are unlearned, but they know when He shows up. They can sense it.

Years ago I was in Versailles, France, doing a concert on a Sunday morning. I was singing in English, but I noticed a young woman in the back who was sobbing through most of the concert. Observing her, I thought to myself, *Wow, the Lord is really dealing with her.* At the end of the concert, I gave an invitation for people to meet Christ and for those needing prayer. She came forward. She told me—through an interpreter, for she apparently did not speak or understand English—that she was Catholic and had never been to a

Protestant service. She then asked me this question: "Why do I keep crying. . . . I can't stop crying. . . . I know you're singing about God, but other than that I cannot understand you. In my heart, I feel I need something. . . . Something is missing. What is this I am feeling?"

I began to relay to her that what she was sensing was God's Holy Spirit. To this she immediately replied, "Quel Saint-Esprit?" As she listened intently to everything I said, I saw her eyes widen as she understood for the first time about God's powerful presence—the presence of Jesus. After praying with her, like so many times on these ministry trips, I felt that I was the one who had learned the most. God's power transcends every language barrier on this earth. She was responding—not to words, but to God's presence that had showed up that day.

God's presence has a way of charging our batteries, refreshing us spiritually, and strengthening us within. I have even gone into worship services where I was already physically drained only to leave revived and renewed. We are charged in His presence. Consequently, our own throne room encounters with God's very real presence will leave us changed, challenged, and charged. There is no other experience in the world like it.

Proclaiming His Praises

As believers, we are called to proclaim the praises of the One who has changed our lives. The more time we spend in His presence, the clearer our purpose will be, the cleaner our hearts will be, and the more powerful our witness will be. Throne room encounters will radically transform us as individuals, and as His people. They will take us from where we are right now to where He's called us to be. The purpose in *proclaiming* His praises is to call others to worship the one true God. God's kingdom is advanced through our worship. Our worship sustains a base of operation for God to work in and through our lives.

> But you are a chosen race, a royal priesthood,
> a holy nation, a people for His possession,
> *so that you may proclaim the praises*
> *of the One who called you out of darkness*
> *into His marvelous light.*
> (1 Peter 2:9, emphasis added)

> *Our worship sustains a base of operation for God to work in and through our lives.*

The Greek word for "proclaim" is *euangelizo*, which means to publish, celebrate, proclaim, report, or praise. It is not a coincidence that in these last days, as we see the broadcasting, publishing, and proclaiming of praise and worship music at an unprecedented pace, we also see the church growing around the world at a rapid pace as well. Doesn't that make sense? As the redeemed proclaim the praises of the One responsible for their redemption, it awakens a hunger in the hearts of others to know Him personally too. "If I am lifted up from the earth, I will draw all [people] to Myself" (John 12:32).

You may or may not know that the root of the Hebrew word transliterated *hallelu* means "to cause to shine." Combine that with "jah" on the end—which is the shortened version of God's name—and we see a word picture of our praises casting the spotlight on the Lord! And that is exactly what 1 Peter 2:9 is talking about. Our worship of Jesus Christ as the only One worthy of all worship and praise will cause the brightness of who He is to shine in our homes, cities, and across the nations.

We don't need to get bogged down in whether or not God likes fast songs or slow songs, whether or not He prefers that we lift our hands from our sides or in the air, whether He likes the piano and organ, or guitars, bass, and drums. You know the answer. All of these things are style. Every congregation, every person is going to have a unique style and way of doing things. Never confuse style with substance. We are called to lift Him up in any way we can. As long as we are lifting up the praises of Jesus, that's what counts to Him and to this hurting world.

It is the *essence* of our worship, not its style, that matters most to the One we praise. Worship is not a formula—true worship will always be an expression of the heart. God responds to the cries of our hearts, whether they are lifted up with a shout or a whisper. True worship will always be taking place when Jesus is the audience for those worshiping. It's not about us, it's about Him—it has always been about Him. He wants to hear your voice. He needs to hear your voice, and you and I need to hear His.

Childlike or Childish

God has called us to be *childlike*, not *childish*. We are to come with no defense, no walls, and no reservations. And should we have any, the Holy Spirit will begin to melt and soften our hearts as He draws us closer to the flame of His presence. We must watch out for the stumbling blocks that the enemy will throw in our path on our way to a greater understanding of praise and worship. They come in the form of dead religion, judgmentalism, secret sin, pride, ignorance, and fear.

We must continually allow the Holy Spirit to probe the depths of our being and yield to His promptings. We want God to be able to flow through our lives unimpeded. We are the glove, He is the hand. We are the channel, He is the flow. We are the conduit, He is the current.

Let us be clear: the Holy Spirit *never* draws attention to Himself; He always points the way to Jesus. It is the anointing that makes the difference. It is the anointing in worship that breaks the yoke of bondage. That's why many times people are healed inside and out in a "worship experience" where God's presence is being manifested.

> Worship is not a formula— true worship will always be an expression of the heart.

Also, there are many physical reactions to the power and presence of God. Some will weep and cry, others will be filled with great joy and a gift of faith, others feel a deep sense of peace and calm come over their troubled minds, while still others get goose bumps or the hair on their arms stands up as He draws near. Many people explain feeling warmth over a certain area of their body, which can sometimes be an area of sickness or disease being healed. Others simply feel overwhelmed by His presence.

Furthermore, and an entire study all by itself, is the fact that praise and worship routs enemy forces. The spirit of heaviness lifts off when the garment of praise is put on. The spirit of fear has nowhere to abide when God instills a sense of victory within our hearts. It's almost too much to take in when you stop and think about all the things that can happen during a time of worship.

Let me put this question to you: why would anyone think these things are strange? Wouldn't you expect something to take place when the God of the universe shows up in power to inhabit your praise? Shouldn't we expect people to be healed in His presence? Don't you think it's time we realize that all things are possible with God? Could it be that the reason we don't see more of this is because somehow we've determined that it doesn't fit in the tiny little box of our limited experience and, thus, because we weren't raised with these kinds of things, they can't be real?

Isn't it time we admit that we don't know it all and that we haven't arrived, and that God is big enough to do something that we've never seen and may never understand—and that He doesn't need nor does He seek our permission to do it? Of course, He wants our cooperation because of how it will change us inside—but if we should refuse, He will find a willing heart somewhere else.

We need to adopt a childlike approach to God, where we come with wonder and awe into His presence and have hearts and minds that are wide open to whatever He wants to do and however He chooses to move. Children are trusting, adventurous, and full of love. As adults, we need to strive to keep those childlike qualities alive in us as we walk through a world that is often jaded and cynical toward the things of God.

Undignified

There is a story in 2 Samuel 6 where King David is dancing wildly before the Lord as the ark of the covenant is being brought back to Jerusalem. His wife Michal looks down from the window of the palace and sees him worshiping God in the dance, and the Bible says "she despised him in her heart" (v. 16).

Upon returning home, Michal confronts David about his undignified worship. His reply speaks to us today: "I was dancing before the LORD who chose me over your father and his whole family to appoint me ruler over the LORD's people Israel. I will celebrate before the LORD, and I will humble myself even more and humiliate myself" (2 Sam. 6:21–22). The Bible then shares a chilling detail: "And Saul's daughter Michal had no child to the day of her death" (2 Sam. 6:23).

The Bible doesn't mention things at random—they are there to serve a purpose. It does not say that God struck

Michal with barrenness; it simply tells us that she had no child until the day of her death. What probably happened here was that her despising of her husband's worship cut to the quick of their relationship, and he most likely was never intimate with her again. While there are a lot of things we can learn in this passage, the big picture here is that being critical of someone's worship and passion for the Lord can result in our own unfruitfulness.

We need to be careful not to criticize worship styles that we don't understand or that may not be a part of our experience. Our criticism may keep us from being fruitful in our own worship and hinder God's plan for our lives.

I will admit that I have been in some church services or prayer meetings where people were worshiping and someone's excitement exceeded the norm in the room. Sometimes people get very demonstrative in their expressions of praise and worship to the Lord. Before I castigate something as purely emotional, I need to remember that I am not the Lord, I am not their judge, and, furthermore, I do not know the price paid for their praise. I haven't walked in their shoes. I don't know what they've been delivered from or what they are going through. If I did, I might be running the aisles with them.

As long as our expressions flow from a heart of love toward the Lord, what difference does it make what form our worship takes? You can go to any professional sports game and watch what adults sometimes act like—in public. Talk about undignified! I would certainly rather be undignified for the Lord than on behalf of some sports team. It's good to have emotion and feelings in worship and I have found that the Holy Spirit will take that passion and move us beyond it into another realm. The Holy Spirit elevates our worship beyond our own enthusiasm.

Let us not be afraid to let our love for the Lord find

expression in our worship of and service to our King. We should never apologize for our passion for His presence or our passion for worship or service to Him. To be sure, there will be times when people won't understand the depth of your zeal or the strength of your devotion. Others might think you are just an emotional mystic who is a bit over the edge. That's OK, don't apologize—keep stoking the fires on the altar and keep a white-hot flame burning in your heart for the Lord. You have been set free to worship. Benjamin Disraeli, the British prime minister in the 1870s, said, "Never apologize for showing feeling. When you do so, you apologize for the truth."

> *We need to be careful not to criticize worship styles that we don't understand or that may not be a part of our experience. Our criticism may keep us from being fruitful in our own worship and hinder God's plan for our lives.*

God wants to heal you from the inside out. God wants to touch you from the inside out. God wants to spend time with you. I think many of those within the church could use some healing—physical, emotional, and spiritual—not to mention what it would do for those who are not yet believers.

May our worship be filled with great joy! If the joy of the Lord is to be our strength, we as the people of God need to fill up regularly. A lot of Christians are lacking in joy. Joy is found in His presence, and when we spend time in His presence, our praise and worship and our very lives will be full of joy.

God sent Moses to Pharaoh with one directive and only one: "Let My people go that they may worship Me." That was it—that's all there was to it. God hungered for the worship of His people. He wanted to hear their praise. God moved heaven and earth to get His people up, out, and into a place where they could worship Him freely. He longed for a relationship with His people. If it was that important then, how much more is it now!

The fruit of your own throne room encounters will be evident in your life and ministry, as His character and likeness has a way of showing up more and more in people who spend time with Him. I want to be around people who spend time in God's presence. There's something different about them that is spiritually attractive. I want to be around people who burn with a passion for God's presence and realize the importance that praise and worship are to have in our lives. I want to be around people who have a heart after God and like David are not afraid to show it. How about you?

God, create a clean heart for me
and renew a steadfast spirit within me.
Do not banish me from Your presence
or take Your Holy Spirit from me.
Restore the joy of Your salvation to me,
and give me a willing spirit.
Then I will teach the rebellious Your ways,
and sinners will return to You. (Ps. 51:10–13)

Chapter 12

Power to Worship

§ § §

William Temple, a former Archbishop of Canterbury, said, "To worship is to quicken the conscience by the holiness of God, to feed the mind with the truth of God, to purge the imagination by the beauty of God, to open the heart to the love of God, to devote the will to the purpose of God."[1]

Probably no other biblical passage exemplifies this better than Isaiah's worship encounter found in Isaiah 6:1–13. We have already discovered that this was Isaiah's throne room encounter, but there is much more to find in this passage. In it we find the classic worship pattern—a Scriptural pattern that can be followed today. There are five distinct stages within Isaiah's worship encounter.

> In the year that King Uzziah died, I saw the Lord seated on a high and lofty throne, and His robe filled the temple. Seraphim were standing above Him; each one had six wings: with two he covered his face, with two he covered his feet, and with two he flew. And one called to another:
>
> Holy, holy, holy is the LORD of Hosts;
> His glory fills the whole earth.

The foundations of the doorways shook at the sound of their voices, and the temple was filled with smoke.

Then I said:
Woe is me, for I am ruined,
because I am a man of unclean lips
and live among people of unclean lips,
[and] because my eyes have seen the King,
the LORD of Hosts.

Then one of the seraphim flew to me, and in his hand was a glowing coal that he had taken from the altar with tongs. He touched my mouth [with it] and said:
Now that this has touched your lips,
your wickedness is removed,
and your sin is atoned for.

Then I heard the voice of the Lord saying:
Who should I send?
Who will go for Us?
I said:
Here I am. Send me.
And He replied:
"Go! Say to these people: . . ." (Isa. 6:1–9)

Five Stages of a Worship Encounter

First Stage (vv. 1–4): Isaiah has a vision of the Lord enthroned amidst the praises of heaven. Immediately *he recognizes God's awesome glory, holiness, and* power. The Hebrew word for *holy* in verse 3 means separated and unapproachable. The Hebrew word for *glory* means God's authority, greatness, and weighty presence. His vision includes the bigness, vastness, and perfection of who God is in comparison with himself.

Second Stage (v. 5): Isaiah, having received the revelation of God's perfection, is undone in God's presence and quickly *recognizes and acknowledges his own sinful condition.* All of his imperfections, all of his shortcomings, all of his uncleanness are glaringly apparent in the light of God's holiness.

Third Stage (vv. 6–7): Having recognized his sinful condition, Isaiah *humbles himself in the presence of the Lord and confesses his sins* to God, and God opens the avenue of cleansing and forgiveness. Confession always opens the way to God's grace and mercy. Only God can provide the purity He demands, through the blood of Jesus.

Fourth Stage (v. 8a): After Isaiah is forgiven and cleansed from his sin, *the Lord shares His need for a messenger.* God will only use cleaned vessels. God will only entrust His will and heart's desires to those who eagerly confess their faults.

Fifth Stage (v. 8b): Having heard the Lord's call for someone to go on His behalf, Isaiah, answering from a clean heart, *responds with, "Here I am. Send me."* Only after his cleansing did he receive his calling (God's will for his life).

This five-stage pattern of a worship encounter with God has never changed. And it is the Holy Spirit within and without that becomes the spiritual energy source that makes such an encounter possible. He makes God's presence real to us while at the same time He is prompting our hearts from within to offer up our very lives to the Lord in loving, surrendered worship.

Worship: Revelation and Response

Worship is receiving God's revelations—whether private, public, or through Scripture—and then responding to it. Worship is revelation and response. We are to "hear the Word" (revelation) and "do the Word" (response). For worship to occur, there must be a response to God. If there is no response from us, then worship has not really taken place. Worship is a two-way street.

God still reveals His will for our lives through worship encounters. Those who are tender toward the Lord will still respond. True worshipers do not have to beg God to reveal His will to them because His will is made apparent during the worship encounters they have with God. True worship is a lifestyle of revelation and response—it is heart worship.

> *True worship is a lifestyle of revelation and response—it is heart worship.*

Whether in the car, at home, work, or church, God is always speaking. The key is—are we listening? Are we responding? Do we keep our hearts open?

Worship Stimuli

Re-read the definition of worship from William Temple, the former Archbishop of Canterbury: "To worship is to quicken the conscience by the holiness of God, to feed the mind with the truth of God, to purge the imagination by the beauty of God, to open the heart to the love of God, to devote the will to the purpose of God."

Let's look at this more closely:

- Quicken our consciences with God's holiness (attributes): This involves fear and reverence for the Lord. God is omnipotent, omniscient, and omnipresent.
- Feed our minds with God's truth (Scripture): We renew our minds with the Word of God.
- Purge our imaginations with God's beauty (creation): The earth is the Lord's, and everything in it. We fill our minds with the splendor of all He has created— from the stars to a baby's first cry.

- Open our hearts to God's love (Jesus): God so loved this world that He gave His One and Only Son.
- Devote our wills to God's purpose (Holy Spirit): Worship reveals God's will to us and makes known to us God's plan and direction.

Worship is receiving revelation through what I'll call "worship stimuli" and then responding to it. Isaiah's heart was stimulated by what he saw in the spiritual realm, what he heard, what he sensed. We too should allow ourselves to be moved by the grandeur and vastness of God and recognize just how small and feeble we are.

Our worship begins in our spirits and moves to our souls (mind, will, & emotions); then it is followed by a physical response to God's presence through our bodies (actions).

Let Him speak to you through the stained glass. Let Him speak to you through the beauty of the earth. Let Him speak to you through the sacraments, through a song of praise, through His Word. Let Him speak to you as you bow before Him. He has a way of showing up if you'll let Him. When we brush against His holiness, we sense how sinful and carnal we are, and immediately we should respond with confession and repentance. In turn, God will provide grace and mercy and cleansing through the shed blood of Jesus. Thus, with cleaned hearts we can hear His call more clearly and respond, as Isaiah did, "Here I am. Send me."

"God is spirit, and those who worship Him must worship in spirit and truth" (John 4:24). Man is spirit; he has a soul, and lives in a body. Jesus told us that the Father is seeking worshipers who will worship Him in spirit and in truth. Our worship begins in our spirits and moves to our souls (mind, will, and emotions); then it is followed by a physical response to God's presence through our bodies (actions). All of these emanate from and are based on absolutes—biblical truth. Our worship is an outward expression of an inward work and it is in sync with God's nature, for God is spirit.

Everywhere you are, He is. There is no place you can go that He is not already there. There is no stain so deep that His blood cannot cleanse. There is no doubt you have that He cannot conquer. Worship Him with all your heart. Love the Lord, your God, with all your heart, mind, soul, and strength.

Public and Private

These thoughts on worship stimuli hold true for both personal and corporate worship. The worship service of the church many times parallels our own personal worship times with the Lord. Awhile back I came across this description from Donald P. Hustad:

The worship service is a rehearsal for life. It outlines the dialogue which goes on constantly between God and believers, giving God's Word and suggesting the response He wants to hear— response which includes our adoration, our confession, our thanksgiving, our dedication, and our petition.

Worship also offers us an opportunity to give ourselves to God in all of life; in token of this, in the worship service we give Him our attention as He speaks to us, we give Him our praise and adoration, we give Him our offerings of money and also of our service in ministry.

Finally, worship is becoming like God in our total personhood—body, emotions, mind, and will. The worship service allows us to exercise every part of ourselves, in order that our bodies might be God's temple, that our spirit might be moved by His Spirit, that our mind might be the mind of Christ, and that our will might be one with the will of God.

True worship then is really all there is to being a Christian, and the worship service is important because of what it represents as a microcosm.[2]

Our worship really becomes the sum total of our lives lived out to God. It is our response to Him and His Word and His will. Worship must come first. Everything we do must flow out of our worship encounters with God, so that everything we do becomes worship to Him. His manifested presence is what I need and seek. In His presence I find the fullness my life needs. If I'm not accessing His presence, then I will lack clarity in my sense of purpose (God's call), sense of direction (God's will), and the fulfillment (God's blessing) that comes from spending time with Him.

> *Our worship really becomes the sum total of our life lived out to God. It is our response to Him and His Word and His will.*

His Dwelling Place: My Home

"LORD, I love the house where you dwell, the place where Your glory resides" (Ps. 26:8). As much as God is "at home" in our praises, I have found that I am most "at home" in His presence—whether it's in a physical church structure somewhere, or beneath His shadow as He tabernacles over me while I praise Him on my own. The physical place doesn't matter to Him or me. I have felt His presence seated within the stone walls of Notre Dame Cathedral, and I have felt His presence driving my car. I want to be where He is. I love His dwelling place—the place where He abides.

If my lot in life were to be but a doorkeeper to His presence, then so be it. What better place to spend my days? When you love His habitation, He will see a heart after Him. When you hunger for the manifestation of His glory, He will see a heart after Him. I want a heart after God, and I am not ashamed to tell Him that if all I get to do is hold the door open to His presence then I am the most blessed of persons.

Better a day in Your courts
than a thousand [anywhere else].
I would rather be at the door of the house of my God
than to live in the tents of the wicked. (Ps. 84:10)

To be "at the door" is to stand at the threshold. That is certainly what I want to do. One day with Him is better than a thousand without Him. I pray that we would all desire to stand at the threshold of God's presence; and through our worship, our brokenness, our repentance, our prayers, our praise, stand in that doorway and keep it open so that God will have a channel through which His glory can flow to others.

I want others to benefit from my praise and worship as it shines the light on the One who has called me out of darkness. I want to lift Him up, exalt Him, extol Him, laud Him, honor Him, glorify Him, thank Him, praise Him, and worship Him. I want to be in the place where His glory resides. I want to be wherever He is. I want to be found at His feet.

A Decision to Make

You and I have a decision to make. Do we want to move out into the depths of all that God has for us? Do we want to venture out into the depths of fresh worship where the Holy

Spirit is leading? Are we tired enough of the "same old, same old" to the point where we have become restless? Will we now allow that holy restlessness to move us up, out, and into what God is doing? While recognizing and honoring what God *has* said, are our ears hungry to hear what God *is* saying? These are not easy questions, and the answers to them will have consequences, whatever we decide.

> *God is looking for people who are sold out to Him.*

Personally, I don't want to be a professional worship connoisseur and mistakenly think I've "arrived" and experienced everything there is to experience in God. How foolish I would be. I want to be a lifelong student of the presence of God. I want to come with a clean slate and say, "Teach me Your ways." What kind of fun is there in playing it safe? Where would the patriarchs, prophets, and disciples have ended up had they played it safe? God is looking for people who are sold out to Him.

Life Is Found Where the River Flows

Once I was with some friends in Bern, Switzerland, and they wanted me to go tubing with them on the River Aare. The River Aare has an unusual and very distinct pale green color, which comes from glacial silt that is carried from its headwaters in the Alps. I had observed this beautiful river numerous times from a distance, from the surrounding hills, from the bridges, etc., but never up close. It was a hot August day, so we descended down the hillside to a place where we could rent our inner tubes and launch safely out into the river.

When we arrived at the water's edge, the first thing I noticed was how fast the river was moving—a lot quicker than it seemed when I had looked at it from the bridges overhead. My Swiss friend, who did this all the time, quickly jumped onto his inner tube and left me on the shallow bank. By the time I jumped in he was already headed down the river. I yelled at him and asked him why I wasn't moving so fast. He replied, "Get away from the bank. Move out into the middle. . . . The current will pick you up!" With the secret firmly in my grasp, I maneuvered out away from the shallows into the flow. And did it work? Wow! What an incredible rush as the current picked me up and began to move me rapidly downstream.

And isn't that the way all the things of God are like? Even worship—getting away from the safety of the shallows and launching out into the flow and allowing Him to take us to where we are supposed to be.

> As the man went out east with a measuring
> line in his hand, he measured off a third of a mile
> and led me through the water. It came up to [my]
> ankles. Then he measured off a third [of a mile] and
> led me through the water. It came up to [my] knees.
> He measured off another third [of a mile] and led
> me through [the water]. It came up to [my] waist.
> Again he measured off a third of a [mile], and it
> was a river that I could not cross [on foot]. For the
> water had risen; it was deep enough to swim in, a
> river that could not be crossed [on foot].
> He [the Lord] asked me, "Do you see [this], son
> of man?" (Ezek. 47:3–6)

In this passage, Ezekiel is addressing a hurting people with the promise of a river that will bring healing and life. In just over a mile, this river increases in depth four times. At each stage the river gathers volume and force. It is a mighty river that digs its own channel and makes its own way. It is not a picture of a sluggish river that will meander along any old traditional rut that is provided for it. This river is a river that will drive itself through the heart of a mountain if necessary rather than fail to arrive at its destination. This river must find the sea or make one. This is a river whose source is God's Holy Spirit.

Let's look at these four stages of the river to help our understanding of worship.

Stage 1: Ankle-Deep

Ankle-deep water represents people who want to be in control of their destiny. They want to stay close to the shore in case of an unexpected wave so they can get out quick. Ankle-deep water is a safe place for people who are afraid of water because they've never been around it or experienced it.

Ankle-deep worship sounds something like, "Praise you, Lord, for meeting my needs and supporting me. Bless me." This is an infant stage—and that's OK. We all have to start somewhere, and this is where we begin to learn to worship. People at this stage tend to be a bit more concerned about what people will think of their worship. They are satisfied with getting their feet wet.

Stage 2: Knee-Deep

Knee-deep water represents people who want a bit more but still want to be in control. They can experience more of how it feels and yet stay within safe reach of the riverbank. People at this stage begin to understand that God wants them to do something with their lives—not just be saved.

Knee-deep worship sounds something like, "Praise You, Lord, for not only watching over me but watching over my family and friends and meeting their needs as well. Make me a better person." This person has grown to the point where he understands that God will meet his needs and becomes more comfortable—his prayers now include concern for others.

Stage 3: Waist-Deep

Waist-deep water represents people who want more. In waist-deep water you can really feel the current pulling at you—you're about to slip in. It's hard to stand still because the current keeps teasing you, pulling at you, beckoning you to yield to it. Though you can still see the riverbank, it is not your focus. You become more intrigued by the adventure of what lies out in the middle of the river.

Waist-deep worship sounds something like, "Praise You, Lord, for meeting my needs and the needs of others. Lord, make me more like You. Lord, thank You for Your power." Here we see someone becoming truly committed. She has learned to put childish things away and become childlike. She now wants the Lord to use her to reach and minister to others. She finds joy in God using her, and the benefits of worship are now becoming very important to her.

Stage 4: Over-Your-Head-Deep

Over-your-head-deep water represents people who have surrendered to the flow. You have ceased to care what people think of your passion and hunger for God. By this time you've lost all sense of knowing or caring where the riverbank is. By this time it's all or nothing. You've been swept into the moving current. The current of God now determines the direction and course of where you go.

Over-your-head-deep worship sounds something like, "Jesus, have Your way in me. Oh, Lord, thank You for Your presence!" Here you get lost in worship, you forget where you are and are simply enjoying the flow of God's presence.

Get Away from the Riverbank

Friend, you cannot remain in ankle-deep water and get all that God has for you. You cannot stay in the wading pool of the Spirit, where it barely touches your knees, and expect to be filled with all that God has for you. Don't be content with waist-deep water, either, if you really hunger for God's presence. You've got to get away from the riverbank and get out into the flow.

Go ahead and get out there where it's over your head, where you have to trust God totally. Get away from the riverbank and the temptation to try to control everything and launch out into the flow where you yield completely to His plan for your life. You will never know what the power of worship can do if you play it safe along the edge. The River will take you to the greatest depths of His love and power as you daily yield to the Spirit of God. God, help us not to anchor to the riverbank of our own ideas, circumstances, and plans. We want to be out in the middle of that current.

> *Go ahead and get out there where it's over your head, where you have to trust God more. Get away from the riverbank and the temptation to try to control everything and launch out into the flow where you yield completely to His plan for your life.*

We all start at "Stage 1," but whether or when we move on to the next stage is up to us. God is calling us all to get out into the middle of the river where the current will take us to where He's purposed us to be. Worship teaches us to yield to what God is saying and what God is doing. The Holy Spirit gives us the power, the resources, the fortitude, the determination, the perseverance to say *yes* our whole life through.

How precious is Your lovingkindness, O God!
Therefore the children of men put their trust
under the shadow of Your wings.

They are abundantly satisfied
  with the fullness of Your house.
And You give them drink
  from the river of Your pleasures.
For with You is the fountain of life;
In Your light we see light.
(Ps. 36:7–9 NKJV, emphasis added)

At the end of Ezekiel's vision, God asked him a question: "Do you see this, son of man?" In other words, "You haven't seen anything yet!" No matter how great or how wonderful our times with the Lord and in the Lord have been up to now, there's certainly more where that came from. I believe we haven't seen anything yet. God is about to unleash His glory on this earth in a way we've not seen before, and it will be carried aloft on the praises of His people. If I were you, I'd get my inner tube and head for the river.

Allow the Holy Spirit to extend and expand your understanding and experience in worship. Plunge into the headwaters of praise and allow yourself to be carried into the flow of the river of the Spirit's anointing as you worship the King and encounter Him. Ask Him now to anoint you with power—Power to Worship!

Final Thoughts

§ § §

I hope that in some small way I have been able to encourage you in your worship of the King. As I have shared from my own experiences, perhaps the Lord has ignited a fire within you that will result in a passion and hunger for His presence. My own walk with the Lord and worship of Him, like yours, is a journey—a journey that I am still walking, constantly learning and unlearning. It is fluid, active, and dynamic. I will never "arrive."

Johann von Goethe, a German playwright of the eighteenth and early nineteenth centuries, said, "We are shaped and fashioned by what we love." What do you love? Who do you love? We will always reflect what we are beholding in our hearts. I pray that you and I will reflect the Lord Jesus Christ, and should there come a time when we do not reflect Him as we should, may we find mercy and forgiveness at His feet.

Behold Him and be in awe of Him, for even though we are privileged to call Him Friend, He is still the Ancient of Days, the Alpha and Omega, the Amen, the Anchor behind the Veil, the Daystar, the Good Shepherd, the Son of Man, the Son of God, Counselor, Mighty God, Prince of Peace, Everlasting Father, Savior, Bread of Heaven, Bright and Morning Star, the Lily of the Valley, the Rose of Sharon,

Master, Advocate, Lamb of God, the Resurrection and the Life, Chief Cornerstone, Immanuel, Living Water, the Word made flesh, Lion of the Tribe of Judah, the Door, the Great High Priest, Redeemer, and the I AM.

We will continue to write about Him, sing about Him, paint pictures about Him, and create art about Him because we will never exhaust our Subject. The unlimited creativity of the Holy Spirit will continue to find expression in and through those who are in love with Jesus Christ. When His presence shows up, we should respect and honor it and give God room to move as He wishes.

Keep Your Hands Up

If I had to use one passage of Scripture that best fits my heart's desire it would be this:
One thing I have desired of the LORD,
That will I seek:
That I may dwell in the house of the LORD
All the days of my life,
To behold the beauty of the LORD,
And to inquire in His temple.
For in the time of trouble
He shall hide me in His pavilion;
In the secret place of His tabernacle
He shall hide me;
He shall set me high upon a rock. (Ps. 27:4–5 NKJV)

I want to seek His face—His presence—continually. God's presence is what I treasure most because His presence is what makes the difference in our lives, in our ministries, in our church services. His presence is His anointing, and it breaks the yoke of bondage over us and others. If He didn't show up, what would we do?

Psalm 31:20 says that God hides us in the protection, the secret place of His presence. There is something very comforting about the "secret place" that is only revealed to those who are in the Lord. Psalm 91:1 assures us that any one of us who chooses to dwell "in the secret place of the Most High" (NKJV) shall be able to abide under the shadowing presence of Almighty God. Where do we find this "secret place" of His presence?

I grew up in a house with a basement. Anytime we went downstairs, we had to go through a little routine in order to turn the lights on. We didn't have a master switch at the top of the steps that could turn all the lights on before we descended the stairs. That would have been too easy. We had to go downstairs in the dark, and once we reached the bottom step, the adventure would begin. As a kid this was a daunting task, especially at night.

The next step was to raise our hands in the air as far as we could because we knew that there were several pull-strings descending from the light fixtures. The trick was to navigate in the dark toward where we thought the pull-string was. So with hands flailing in the air, I went in the general direction where I knew the light was. I knew that once I found that string all I had to do was pull, and voila, light. It was like finding a secret in the dark. I knew it was there, but I was so proud of myself when I found that silly string.

Now I have a house of my own, and sure enough, in the back of our basement, we still have one of those dreaded pull-strings. Only now, I not only have to navigate through the basement in the dark with my hands in the air, I have to be careful where I step, as I usually trip over a toy or two left by my kids. One night, as I was walking circumspectly through the basement with my outstretched hands flailing in darkness, I thought how silly I must look if someone could have seen me doing my basement routine, searching for the pull-string.

It was then that I realized that finding the "secret place" of God's presence is a bit like my looking-for-the-pull-string basement routine. You see, we know God is there but we enter "there" with hands uplifted. We enter the darkness— the unknown—trusting in Him. Our hands are raised in full surrender, and they are raised because we are intent on finding the pull-string. We know it's there, it's just a matter of homing in on it.

There in my basement I thought to myself, I can't even count how many times I have gone through this silly little routine: walking in the darkness slowly with my hands held high, feeling for the string from the light. God, of course, is not hiding from us or keeping Himself from us on purpose; He is always there waiting for us—waiting to be found. Once we find Him, we act so surprised and we are so happy, but it's because we are looking for Him on purpose that we find joy and bring Him great joy as well. We are intent on finding the light and we find it.

I want to go through my life with my hands in the air. My hands in the air signify several things. First, I am not in a defensive posture—I am actually quite vulnerable with hands lifted up in surrender. Second, my outstretched arms signify my faith that I know that God is there in that situation and He will be found in the midst of it. Third, walking into the unknown with my hands up reminds me that I cannot always see what is going on beforehand, but I know that God is there and that He will never leave me alone. I learn to trust as I walk into the unknown with my hands lifted in praise. I am, in effect, praising Him in advance for what He's going to do.

There is power for worship found in the experiences of the unknown. There is power for worship found in the exercise of seeking Him. There is power for worship found in the darkness, for even in the shadows He is there. Anywhere He shows up, that atmosphere is right for a worship encounter. Keep your hands up. Look for the pull-string, and when you find it, you know what to do; pull, for you have found the "secret place." *Worship hard!*

I'd Rather Dwell (Psalm 84)
Words & Music: David M. Edwards*

Verse 1:
I'd rather dwell in the house of the Lord
Than to dwell in the tents of the wicked
I'd rather be a keeper of the door
To Your presence...
I'd rather walk within the sound of Your voice
Than to never hear You speak
Just let me stay—stay right here with You

Chorus:
O let me live near Your altar
O let me live in Your temple
Where one day is better than a thousand
Where one day is better than a thousand
Without You

Verse 2:
I'd rather fall before Your throne
Than bow before any other god
I'd rather sit at Your nail-scarred feet
And worship You alone...
I'd rather rest in the warmth of Your love
Than to wander aimlessly
Just let me stay—stay right here with You

About the Author

§ § §

David M. Edwards is a man driven. Driven by a passion to see people enter into the presence of God. Driven to see (and be a part of) a new generation of seekers—seekers after the face of God, and not just the "hands" of God. David has had a lifetime full of experiences—shaping him into the teacher/writer/pastor/worshiper that he is today. His music and teaching ministry has taken him to places as far away as France, Germany, Switzerland, Romania, and the United Kingdom—as well as all over America.

David and his wife Susan and their three children have been in ministry for fifteen years. New songs of worship have been pouring out of him for years. David has worked with prolific songwriters such as Margaret Becker, Ginny Owens, Chris Eaton, Steve Hindalong, Greg Nelson, Natalie Grant, Matt Brouwer, Caleb Quaye, and John Hartley. "These songs are all about Him—they're not about me," David relates. "Pain teaches us to worship and cling to God, so my songs come from personal experience and pain in my own life. There's always something we can be grateful for—to come to God and thank Him."

In 2003, David began "Power to Worship Encounter"—a seminar where attendees not only learn about the "nuts and bolts" of worship, but experience God's presence as well.

This book developed out of the overwhelmingly positive response to those seminars. David's desire is for people to be ministered to as well as perfect their craft and calling. In 2005, he was awarded *Worship Leader Magazine*'s "Best Scripture Song" Praise Award for his song "Create in Me" off his *Faithfully Yours: Psalms* project with Margaret Becker. Four *Season of . . .* and three *Faithfully Yours . . .* devotional books on worship featuring David's songs and selections from the *Holman Christian Standard Bible,* as well as the new *Holman CSB Worship Bible* edited by David Edwards, will be released in 2006 and 2007.

To find out more about David Edwards's
music, books, and ministry contact:
The Select Artist Group
P.O. Box 1418
LaVergne, TN 37086
www.theselectartistgroup.com
or
www.davidmedwards.com

For more books by David M. Edwards:
www.bhpublishinggroup.com

Notes

§ § §

Chapter 1

1. Quoted in *Paraclete Theological Journal* (Gospel Publishing House) (Summer 1993).

Chapter 3

1. Leo G. Cox, *Beacon Bible Commentary* (Kansas City, MO: Beacon Hill Press, 1969), 1:305.

Chapter 5

1. Sally Morgenthaler, "Worship: The Real Thing," *Worship Leader Magazine* (Nov./Dec. 1995).

Chapter 9

1. The Barna Group, "The Barna Report 1997," www.barna .org/.

2. Frederick Buechner, "Wishful Thinking," An Essay by Frederick Buechner, 1973, Wheaton College Archives and Special Collections, Wheaton, IL.

Chapter 10

1. Gerrit Gustafson, "Worship Evangelism," *Psalmist* magazine, 1998.

Chapter 12

1. William Temple (1881–1944), 98th Archbishop of Canterbury, from a 1944 BBC broadcast, later transcribed in *Anglican Digest* (London, England).

2. Donald P. Hustad, *True Worship: Reclaiming the Wonder and Majesty* (Wheaton, IL: Harold Shaw, 1998).